1978

PEOPLES OF THE EARTH

volume thirteen
China (including Tibet)
Japan and Korea
THE DANBURY PRESS

Contents

Supervisory Editor of the Series:
Professor Sir Edward Evans-Pritchard,
Fellow of All Souls, Professor of Social Anthropology,
University of Oxford, 1946-1970,
Chevalier de la Légion d'Honneur

(Preceding page)
Terraced paddy fields
stretch towards the horizon
in Yunnan, south-west China.
For centuries unknown to the
west, peasants like these
with oxen and wooden plows
fed mighty empires with
their rice crop.

The DANBURY PRESS
a division of GROLIER ENTERPRISES INC.

Publisher
ROBERT B. CLARKE

© 1973 Europa Verlag

Library of Congress Catalog Card No. 72 85614

Printed in Italy by
Arnoldo Mondadori Editore, Verona

STAFF CREDITS
Editorial Director **Tom Stacey**

Picture Director **Alexander Low**
Executive Editor **Katherine Ivens**
Art Director **Tom Deas**
Assistant Editor **Elisabeth Meakin**
Project Co-ordinator **Anne Harrison**
Research **Cheryl Moyer**

Specialist Picture Research **Diana Eggitt**
Picture Research **Claire Baines/Elly Beintema**
Jeanne Griffiths/Carolyn Keay/Emma Stacey
Editorial Assistants **Richard Carlisle/Rosamund Ellis**
J M Marrin/Susan Rutherford/Pamela Tubby
Editorial Secretary **Caroline Silverman**
Design Assistants **Susan Forster, Richard Kelly**
Cartography **Ron Hayward**
Illustrations **Sandra Archibald, Ron McTrusty**

Production **Roger Multon**
Production Editor **Vanessa Charles**

The publishers gratefully acknowledge help from
the following organizations:
Royal Anthropological Institute, London
Musée de l'Homme, Paris
International African Institute, London
British Museum, London
Royal Geographical Society, London
Scott Polar Research Institute, Cambridge
Royal Asiatic Society, London
Royal Central Asian Society, London
Pitt-Rivers Museum, Oxford
Horniman Museum, London
Institute of Latin American Studies, London

PICTURE CREDITS
Cover: **Brian Brake** (The John Hillelson Agency), **Marc Riboud**
(Magnum from the John Hillelson Agency). **Hugh Baker** 96 through
99. Camera Press 78 tr, 133 t. **Marceline de Montmollin** 82 through 87.
Roma Gelder 78 tl & br, 80 c. **Stuart Gelder** 110 bl. **Felix Greene** 104 t,
105, 114 b, 121 tr. **Richard Harrington** (Camera Press) 118 b. **Rune
Hassner** (Tiofoto) 104 b. From the John Hillelson Agency – **Brian
Brake** 18 c, 26 t, 27, 28, 30 t, 30 br, 31 tr, 32 – 33, 34 t, 81. **Anne de
Henning** 68 through 70, 72 – 73, 95. **Dr Georg Gerster** 29 t, 36 tl & cl.
From the John Hillelson Collection – **John Thomson** 122 through 130.
Gamma from the John Hillelson Agency – **Debre-Afi** 102 tl. Magnum
from the John Hillelson Agency – **Bruno Barbey** 18 b, 20, 22 tr & bl,
24 tl. **Ian Berry** 29 c, 40 b, 42 tl & br, 44 through 49. **Rene Burri** 102 –
103 t, 120. **Henri Cartier Bresson** 132 b, 133 b, 134, 135 tl & bl. **Burt
Glinn** 16 – 17, 19, 22 cr, 23, 24 br, 26 b. **Hiroshi Hamaya** 18 t. **Marc
Riboud** 2 – 3, 100 – 101, 103 tr, 104 c, 107, 108 tl, 110 br, 111, 112, 114 tl,
116 – 117, 119, 121 b, 135 r. **Marilyn Silverstone** 64 cl & tr, 65, 88
through 92. **Tony Howarth** (Susan Griggs) 62 – 63. **S. Isaacs** (F.P.G.)
71. **Philip Jones Griffiths** 67t. **Dimitri Kessel** (Life Magazine) 108 c & b,
109. Keystone Press 79 t, 132 t. **Robert Laffont** 79 b. **John Launois**
(Black Star, New York) 24 tr, 64 b, 66, 67 b. **John Launois** (Transworld)
30 cr. **Fred J Maroon** (Louis Mercier) 34 c, 35, 38 – 39. **Fred Mayer**
(Woodfin Camp Associates) 21 b. **Roland Michaud** (Rapho, Paris) 74
through 77, 80 t & br. **Eigi Miyazawa** (Transworld) 34 b, 40 t, 41, 42 cl
& tr. **Robert Pastner** (Black Star, New York) 36 bl. **Robert Pastner**
(Transworld) 36 tr. **Paul Popper** 131 l. Radio Times Hulton Picture
Library 131 r. **Anne-Marie Random** 21 tc. **Harry Redl** 102 bl. **Emil
Schulthess** (Black Star, New York) 110 t, 113, 114 tr & c. Sunday
Times 118t.
Key: **t**=top, **c**=centre, **b**=bottom, **r**=right, **l**=left.

Peoples of the Earth, volumes one to twenty

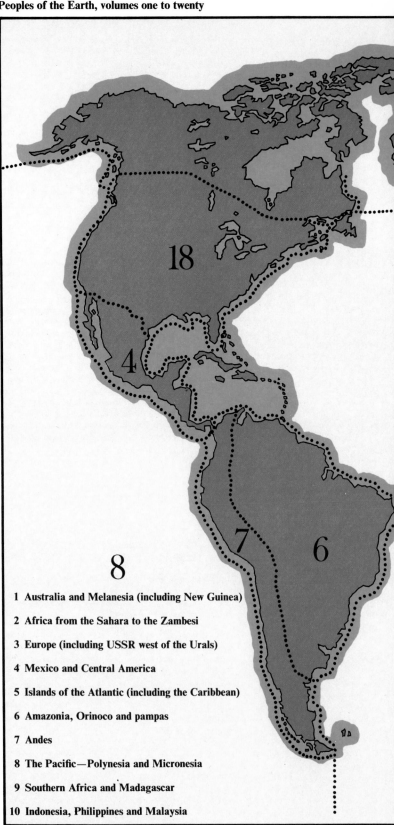

1 **Australia and Melanesia (including New Guinea)**

2 **Africa from the Sahara to the Zambesi**

3 **Europe (including USSR west of the Urals)**

4 **Mexico and Central America**

5 **Islands of the Atlantic (including the Caribbean)**

6 **Amazonia, Orinoco and pampas**

7 **Andes**

8 **The Pacific—Polynesia and Micronesia**

9 **Southern Africa and Madagascar**

10 **Indonesia, Philippines and Malaysia**

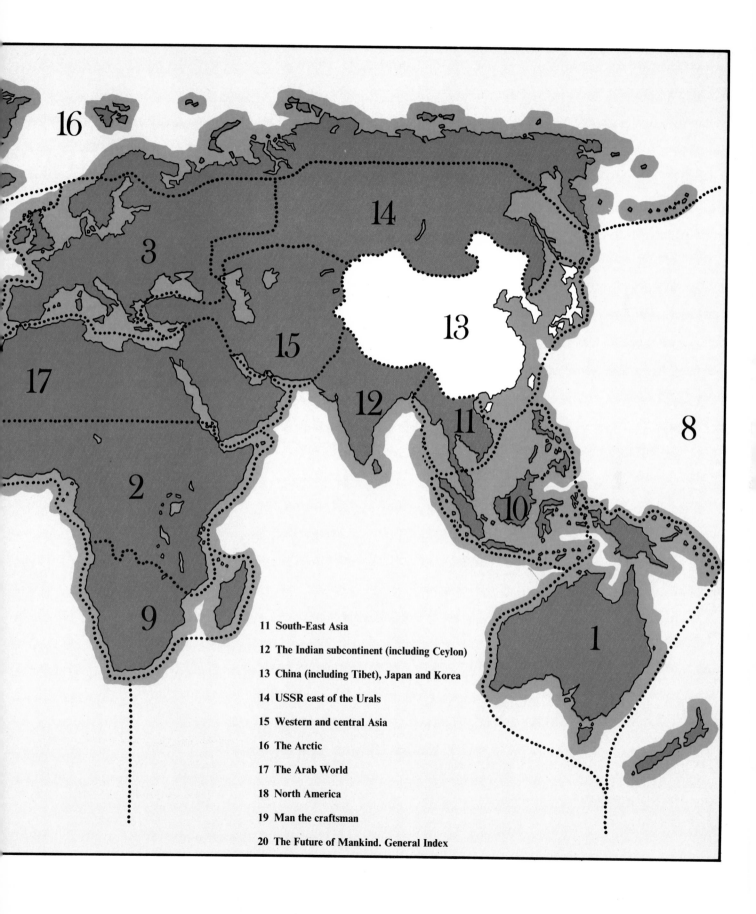

Religion: man and his beliefs

Man is nowhere satisfied with the world of physical appearance, and for good reasons. In most places and at most times human existence has been painful and puzzling. Nature on the one hand displays a basic order. The sun rises and sets. The moon waxes and wanes. The rains come in their due season and the earth is green once more. On the other hand lightning strikes suddenly, perhaps to kill. Or the rains are late and poor, and people go hungry. Disease may strike suddenly as lightning or linger insidiously like starvation. Game becomes scarce. Cattle die. Women are inexplicably barren. These things do not only cause pain and anxiety in themselves. They also seem to contradict what has been discerned of an underlying majestic order. It seems natural, then, to try to understand that order; to seek to relate individual and social experience to it in a meaningful way; to try to rediscover or restore it when it appears to have been shattered by affliction. Although it is natural no other animal, as far as we know, does it. Only man is a pattern-seeker and a pattern-maker. By discovering and creating pattern out of apparent chaos, he tries to tap the powers he feels to be inherent in the universe beyond the world of appearance.

For some 200 years western man has increasingly engaged in empirical pattern-making. It depends on controlled observation, numerical measurements and repeated experiment. Although these patterns or models of the universe which he creates still involve substantial work of the imagination they do consistently seem to fit the puzzling appearances. For people who share in this scientific system of thought, many of the intellectual problems presented by the natural world have at least receded. Scientific techniques have indeed made it possible to tap the hidden powers of the universe. Yet successfully relating human experience in a meaningful way to these powers and to this very fact of life remains an unsolved problem. Many of the seemingly irrational eastern cults of western urban youth seem to be directed towards the same set of questions.

The universal feature of human societies is some kind of symbolic thinking. Mathematical symbols, as a human activity, are limited in space and time. Scientific thinking involves trying to make patterns of reality with mathematical symbols so that as a consequence reality may be manipulated in terms of these symbols. But mathematics in human history is but a recent and sporadic development of symbolic thought.

For most of mankind, for most of history, and in many parts of the earth today, other symbols have been far more readily available. Fire and water. Left and right. The sky and earth. Color and sex. The huge variety of living things. All these symbols are universal and have been used everywhere to build up patterned pictures of the world in different combinations and with many local variants, and to devise means of exerting some sort of control over the powers of the universe.

These material symbols taken from the natural environment can be used directly. They can be physically manipulated through the patterned symbolic action we call rituals. Or they may alternatively be used at one remove, as purely mental counters in building up a system of thought. In this indirect way they can be used to classify all natural phenomena, all the powers of the universe, into categories formed around a few symbols. Or they can be used by telling stories of how the world and human society came to be. Usually all these things interlock. The myth purports to explain the classification of phenomena although it cannot, as a rule, logically be conceived without this classification. Both myth and classification of phenomena justify and validate the ritual. And the ritual in turn re-enacts and reinforces the classifications and the myth.

Ritual does not depend on the material symbols of fire and water *et cetera* alone. Thought and action, intentions and words are at least equally important and often more so. Often the spiritual condition of the man who officiates in the ritual is thought to be crucial for its success. Many religions, for instance, demand a fast or a period of sexual abstinence from the performers of certain rites. Or, as in Christian baptism, the rite may be thought ineffective unless the proper form of words is used.

Using words like 'success' and 'ineffective' implies that a rite is thought to be intended to achieve a definite end – which in baptism, for example, is the admission of either a new-born child or a convert (regarded as born again) into the fellowship of Christian souls. In other rites the intention may be to bring on much-needed rain, or to reconcile longstanding enemies, or to remove an undesirable condition like sickness or barrenness. Many rites are intended to propel people safely through the most important transitions or turning-points of their lives. A good example are the initiation rites of many non-western societies and marriages and funeral ceremonies. Or the ritual may be a periodic all-purpose affair, designed to preserve the order of things rather than restore it with specific objectives of preserving continued good health, peace, prosperity, abundant game, fertility in crops and cattle and women.

The aim in all these rituals is to enlist the help of the powers of the universe. Where the rite is essentially a matter of symbolically manipulating physical objects or substances, the powers of the universe are believed in some way to be transmitted through the objects and substances themselves. Either the material symbols, the objects and substances, may be held to possess in themselves an inherent power, which is at once quickened and controlled by ritual action. Or the whole exercise of ritually manipulating the symbols may be seen as a communication with other, unseen powers, which are in some sense outside the symbols. It is this difference of belief attached to the ritual manipulation of material symbols which is the difference between magic and religion.

Although this difference between magic and religion is real it should not, however, be made into a hard-and-fast dichotomy. There are many languages and cultures which distinguish between magic and religion – and their participants would recognize them as different sorts of activity – but the distinction is by no means universal. Many phenomena in fact lie on the fringe between magic and religion. When a magician addresses a prayer to the medicine he is preparing, or when communicants at a sacrifice believe themselves to be supernaturally invigorated by eating what has been offered to a god, it becomes difficult to draw the line.

Another, related distinction which is also far from universal is sometimes drawn between the sacred on the one hand and the secular or profane on the other. Many religions do in fact distinguish between the ordinary everyday world of common sense and practical action, and the special sphere in which esoteric knowledge and ritual action prevail. This special, sacred sphere of action is often hedged about with restrictions. A man may have to submit to fasting or to sexual restrictions before approaching the sacred. He may have to purify himself by a ceremonial washing, or perhaps by covering his body with ash, or he may have to put on special clothes or ornaments. Whole categories of people – women, uninitiated boys, strangers – are sometimes excluded from participating in certain rites. Or the sacred drama of ritual may take place in some special, consecrated enclosure: a church, temple, mosque or a forbidden grove.

But this distinction between the everyday and the sacred is not universal. Many peoples are constantly surrounded in their daily lives by the material symbols that embody their religious creed. To these people religion is in no sense other-worldly. For them everything that is sacred is also for much of the time secular. Everything natural is also supernatural. These people could hardly conceive of a distinction between the two. It is often to such peoples that all magic is religious magic, and all religion magical.

There is, nevertheless, something in the minimal definition of religion which was given by the Victorian anthropologist, Sir Edward Tylor. He defined religion as a belief in spiritual beings. Whether or not it is possible to define spiritual in a universally satisfactory way religion does imply that the message which is symbolically expressed in ritual is addressed to somebody outside the congregation of worshippers. It implies that the message is being addressed to some powerful being or beings, usually thought invisible to ordinary human eyes, whose favors must be sought or whose anger must, by this means, be averted.

9

Spiritual beings, the recipients of these messages, have been imagined in a bewildering multiplicity of forms. Some of them may be quite humble – as where a magician's spell over his medicine is indistinguishable from a prayer addressed to it, and it is possible to say that the magician is in this case addressing a spiritual being that he thinks of as immanent in the combination of ingredients. This is one of the examples of borderline cases between magic and religion. In many parts of the world, however, people stand in a religious relationship with certain material objects of their environment which are derived from animals or plants. These objects are necessarily the same as the ones used in rituals. Indeed, as often as not, these objects with which people regard themselves in a religious relationship are scrupulously avoided. It is more that the objects or the animals or plants are regarded as in some way representing 'their' people. The fate of 'their' people is bound up with them. This religious relationship to objects is totemism. The object or animal or plant is a totem.

This general notion of a religious relationship with a material totem covers a bewildering variety of beliefs and practices. The totem label is not in fact as useful as it may seem. Societies that practise totemism are possibly most frequently divided into named groups. The members of these named groups, each of which is associated with its own totems, are often recruited by descent either through males or through females. There is often some myth to justify the association of the people with the totem. A totem animal, for example, may be thought in some sense the ancestor of its particular group. Or it may be thought to have helped the original human ancestor or ancestress out of some difficulty. Where the totem is edible the myth associating the totem with the group may then in effect explain the prohibition on the members of the group killing or eating it. Sometimes where there is a diversity of totem species or objects the diversity of totems is used to build up a picture of a world which is divided into different categories of phenomena, each of which is under the aegis of one totem. Then, although this is not universally true of societies with beliefs that feature totemism, the classification of the natural world neatly fits the classification of society into its different groups. The animal-headed gods of ancient Egypt are believed to have originated in totem deities. And the fabulous animals of European heraldries may represent the last traces of a prehistoric totemism. In India it is certain castes that are reputed to have totems. As castes tend to be defined by occupation, their totems – appropriately – are cultural artifacts like the needle and the wheel.

Another widespread belief endows the dead with an after-life and power over the living. Indeed the dead are often endowed with far more power than they could have exercised in life. Sometimes the dead with this power are a collective, undifferentiated mass of ghosts, who require at most a collective propitiation. In other cases important named ancestors watch over their children. These ancestors are quick to punish any neglect in the duty of remembrance or offering, and also any anti-social behavior likely to disrupt the group formed by their descendants. A totem may be regarded as a kind of ancestor. And more ordinary ancestors may, as they have become to some extent depersonalized, supra-individual guardians of the group's welfare, in turn resemble totems. Often the ancestors also guard their group's moral values. Actions like incest and bloodshed within the group may be forbidden because the ancestors would be angry. Ancestral anger could result in illness and misfortune. Ancestor worship tends to be most important where descent is the basic principle by which society is ordered. Traditional China and ancient Rome, as well as many contemporary African societies, are good examples. But the Nuer of the southern Sudan, who are often cited as a typical example of a society organized by descent groups, have no ancestor cult.

Important ancestors, like certain totems, often have explanatory myths attached to them. This is particularly true of royal ancestors and those ancestors whose descendants form a fairly large political unit like a tribe. These explanatory myths attached to ancestors may relate how the ancestor first came to the country where his descendants now live. They may tell how he crossed rivers and mountains, overcame men and monsters, married beautiful women and founded his descent group. He is often credited with the invention of important tools and techniques, or with the institution of some sacred custom. He is even, in a few cases, credited with having participated in the creation of the world. Culture-heroes of this type are often rather less moralistic figures than more immediate forefathers. To overcome the preter-natural dangers and create a society calls for strength and cunning rather than strictly ethical behavior. Culture-heroes are often also tricksters.

If ancestors shade off into culture-heroes, culture-heroes shade off into gods. These too may have varying degrees of importance: from the deities that protect small localized groups, through nature-spirits that inhabit tree, rock and stream, deities of the forest, agriculture, iron, female fertility, sun, moon, stars, thunderstorms or widely prevalent diseases, to great Earth Goddesses and Sky Gods, sometimes thought of as forming a divine parental couple from which all living things have sprung. The ritual worship of the gods, culminating perhaps in blood sacrifice, brings together congregations of varying size and it enshrines myths that account for the differentiation of cosmos out of chaos, or, more simply, the importance in human life of what the gods stand for. Smallpox may be seen as the anger of a neglected goddess. Heaven and Earth may be believed to have once been close together, until the disobedience of a woman forced them apart. The scale on which the gods are imagined generally reflects not only the size of the phenomena they account for, but also the size of the social group that worships them. A local grove-spirit need affect only a few dozen people, but Earth and Sky deities are, at least potentially, gods for all mankind.

Many gods, like the trickster culture-heroes, are little concerned with ethics. The Earth, however, when she is worshipped, is often an exception. She has received the bodies of the ancestors, who are *par excellence* the guardians of morality. Incest and bloodshed are therefore often also thought to offend her. The Sky God (or, as he is sometimes called, the High God) is on the other hand apt to be seen as remote and uninvolved, a *deus otiosus*. He may in some sense have made the world, or have been very near to it once, but by now he has lost interest and the mere doings of men hardly concern him. In many societies he receives individual prayers, but little collective ritual attention. He may however be thought of as the ultimate recipient of sacrifices addressed to lesser divinities. The High God shades off into the universalistic Supreme Deity of the monotheistic religions who is much concerned with ethical behavior and is in some cases worshipped with elaborate ritual.

These different strands of religious thought – totemism, ancestor-worship, honored culture-heroes, nature-spirits, gods of all degrees of magnitude and universality – exist in various combinations in cultures that are often widely separated from each other in space and time. The strands can be woven into many different patterns, some incorporating only one or two strands, others many; and the total pattern will be different in each case. The total pattern formed by the various strands of religious thought will vary in complexity and in the relative importance which is given to their different elements. It will vary not only with what creates the pattern – lands and climates and the scale of the particular human society – but also with historical factors of stability and change. Over many centuries stable societies will perhaps evolve religions in which all makes for harmony. The religions will also encourage the individual to fit into his group, the group into the larger community, and the social order into the cosmic order.

In other societies, beset by situations of sudden and bewildering change, harmonious patterns will be inadequate and will be replaced perhaps by an entirely new mythical ideology which will justify and validate ritual efforts to attain an immediate millennium. In a situation where a new mythical ideology is sought there is often scope for the imaginative power and personal charisma of one individual. A 'prophet new inspir'd' can totally change a society's religious outlook, assembling the traditional elements of its symbolic thought into a hitherto unsuspected order, inventing new modes of ritual action that seem to cope more satisfactorily with the vicissitudes of human life. The influence of such a man may extend far beyond the society that gave him birth: the Buddha, Jesus and Mohammed are obvious examples. There have also been more modern prophets among various African and Melanesian peoples, and among some North American Indians. Quests of this kind for a new and meaningful pattern are often seen as a return to the sources, to an uncontaminated religion of long ago, before new and disturbing factors set in. The new movement is never, however, a simple return. New elements of religious thought and action may be introduced, perhaps under old names. Or the pieces of the cosmic puzzle may simply be reassembled, so that the resulting pattern appears to promise a more satisfying solution.

The possibilities of such combinations and recombinations of symbols old and new are practically unlimited. The one truly universal thing about religion is the ceaseless and fruitful activity of man, the pattern-maker.

Peoples of the far east

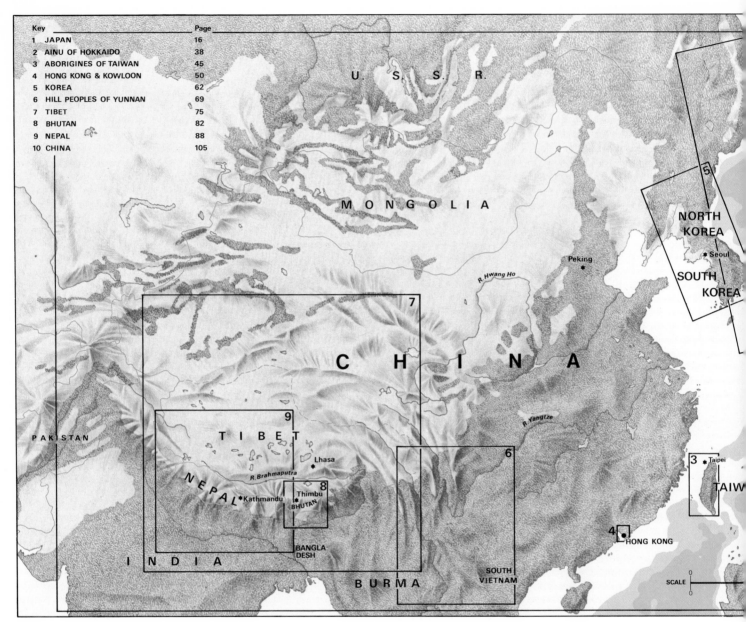

The area covered by this volume is the vast east Asian land mass and the major offshore islands of Taiwan and Japan.

This area can hardly be described as a geographical unity. It is true that its western and south-western borders are marked by the contours of the descent of the Himalayas into the plains of the Indian sub-continent, but there is no clear geographical divide between China and mainland South-east Asia, or between her northern regions and the neighboring states of Mongolia and the USSR. Nor in terms of physical geography is there a case for including in the area the Japanese islands while excluding the island of Sakhalin nearby.

If east Asia is not a geographical unity can we think of it as a unity in terms of its people? This volume shows that we cannot. The contrasts of physical type – between the hairy Ainu in the north of Japan and the smooth-skinned, small-boned people of south China, and between the dark-skinned peoples of Nepal and the big muscular northern Chinese – speak for themselves.

Nor is language a unifying feature. One major linguistic group, the Sino-Tibetan group, certainly predominates in the area, but there are many other languages not of this group, and while some of them are spoken by comparatively few people, it is not possible to ignore the claim to importance of Japanese. Japanese is not even remotely related to the Sino-Tibetan languages.

There are many different styles of life in the area,

ranging from the nomadic through slash-and-burn to the settled agriculturalists, and all manner of customs and dress and social structure. None of these factors encourages us to think of east Asia as a discrete unity.

One feature which does perhaps bind the area together is the dominance of China, for the orientation of the greater part of east Asia was and is towards China. This orientation takes many different forms, but they can probably all be covered under the descriptive heads of political and cultural orientation. Politically other societies of east Asia might be either defensively or offensively orientated towards China. In the first case they have paid tribute and accepted nominal or real Chinese overlordship. In the second they have been covetous of China's wealth and of the power of the rulers. In few cases, either formerly or now, could east Asian societies ignore China. Culturally there has been so much to gain from the Chinese that there is little of east Asia which is not, to some extent at least, in their debt.

The Chinese have always believed themselves to be at

the center of the world. Their word for China ()

means 'the central state'. Around that nub and attracted to it have been the other societies of east Asia and the world. Since Chinese society and culture have been manifestly superior to any of the societies and cultures around them, then it follows that for the Chinese China has come to represent civilization and all else must be considered barbarian. To this view most of the 'barbarians' have tacitly subscribed, though this is not to say that all of them have wished to become 'civilized'.

Here emerges a point which it is not easy for the west to appreciate. Western history teaches us that superior civilizations mark their superiority by proudly attempting to convert to their ways those societies which are considered to be inferior through persuasion or force. Chinese cultural superiority has apparently rarely felt this need for missionary effort. For the Chinese superiority has resulted in a different kind of arrogance, an arrogance which has assumed that such obvious superiority will be admired and desired by the inferior, who will subscribe to it of their own accord. If they do not, then it is clear indication of their inferiority and unworthiness: they do not deserve the benefits of civilization. Even within China itself there have been people considered unfit to possess the full gift of cultural superiority. Consequently women, the sons of prostitutes or actors, boat-dwellers and other unworthies were formerly not permitted to sit for the civil service examinations, the formal channel through which cultural superiority was recognized. Hence, barbarian east Asia could be China-orientated without being converted to Chinese ways.

China has seldom indulged in imperialist wars of conquest. What could be the advantage in ruling barbarians with nothing to offer their rulers? She has been more interested in establishing recognition of her superiority, and therefore a likelihood of peace on her borders through ensuring the existence there of non-hostile buffer-states. East Asia from Nepal to Korea (and indeed parts of South-east Asia too) has for centuries paid tribute in kind to China in recognition of her ascendancy. But even the tribute system was more symbolic than real, for the bearers of tribute were normally sent home by the Chinese emperor with return gifts of higher value than those they had brought with them.

And yet tribute has not always flowed into China. Indeed there have been times when the situation has been reversed and China has herself been forced to pay tribute, notably during the Sung dynasties of the 11th to 13th centuries. China has an unbroken history as a civilization going back to times too remote to be chronicled, but she has not been strong and powerful throughout that period. There have been times when the ruling house has been weak and ineffectual, times when rebellions and de-centralization have thrown the state into chaos, times when invaders have brought her to her knees. The fact that at such times east Asia remained China-orientated and China-influenced points to what really lies behind China's dominance of the area: the quality of her civilization, the power-breeding, wealth-breeding, high culture-breeding potential of her civilization. If at any time China were not strong, it was never a guarantee that she would not be powerful again in the future. If China were not strong, her people were nonetheless the possessors of a form of social organization, of a type of agriculture and settlement, of a proud living historical tradition, and above all of a fund of literacy and technical achievement, which made them the envy and the superiors of all around. It was, in other words, China's cultural supremacy that made her the focus of east Asia. Even in the politically weak Sung dynasty, the philosopher Shao Yung could say 'I am happy because I am a human and not an animal; a male, and not a female; a Chinese, and not a barbarian; and because I live in Loyang, the most wonderful city in all the world.'

Such an attitude, confirmed in its correctness by hundreds of years of contact with peoples who were never the cultural equals of themselves, was sufficient to buoy up the Chinese against whatever adverse political tides might threaten to engulf them. Their unquestioning certainty of their own superiority acted upon the Chinese like a gyroscope: the Chinese state might fall, Chinese culture would remain unshaken. Thus, when China was conquered by another power, it was that other power which changed its ways, adopting Chinese forms of government, Chinese philosophical ideas, the Chinese system of writing, and, in brief, becoming in a very short while Chinese. Within a few decades of establishing its rule over China in the late 17th century, the alien Manchu dynasty was almost completely indistinguishable from a native Chinese dynasty – 'the dog it was that died'.

There is a remarkable difference between the states of the east Asian societies to the east and to the west of China.

To the west is a multiplicity of peoples claiming small pieces of a territory which is so rugged, inhospitable or unproductive that the Chinese have been little interested in it. While very much within the Chinese sphere of influence, these peoples have not on the whole borrowed greatly from the Chinese culture. The Tibetan ruling classes, it is true, adopted some of the tangible products of Chinese culture such as Chinese silks, but they were not greatly influenced in more fundamental ways until the second half of the 20th century. For the other peoples such was their rude state that there was a lack of desire on the part of the Chinese to impart their superior culture, and, probably more important, there was in these societies a complete lack of the social infra-structure which would permit the adoption of Chinese techniques and cultural sophistication. For slash-and-burn Lahu or nomadic Golok horsemen the stable institutions of Chinese society, the schools and the government offices, were out of the question, and similarly the wealth to support a non-productive bureaucracy or scholar class could not be created in the harsh mountainous environments of the Nasi people.

When the western colonial powers arrived in India and South-east Asia the role of these peoples as buffers became even more pronounced. Being within the Chinese sphere of influence they were left alone by the British and French, and consequently they remained as untouched by western civilization as they had been by Chinese culture. The political buffer role has tended to make these peoples cultural museum pieces. Today most of them have come much more firmly under Chinese control, but it is interesting that the Chinese government has made efforts to guarantee a large measure of autonomy to them, and to encourage them to preserve their cultural heritages and identities.

To the east of China there is a quite different picture, for here are found the large and important societies of Korea and Japan. Korea was yet another of the tributary states of China, a state about which the Chinese were much concerned, for as well as paying tribute, the Koreans were subject to further political controls in that China from the 17th century onwards held powers of investiture over the Korean kings. But what chiefly marks out the Koreans and the Japanese from the peoples to the east of China is not their political relationship with China – indeed the Japanese were never in a politically dependent position – but the enormous extent of their cultural borrowings from China.

The kingdom of Paekche in Korea officially adopted Chinese writing in 374 AD and Buddhism spread from China some ten years later. But earliest Chinese contacts there go back to before the Christian era, and the

Koreans have taken in many other cultural features including Confucianism. Today in South Korea, although it is possible to write the language entirely in Korean alphabetic syllable groups, Chinese characters tend to be mixed in with them.

Japan has over many centuries been China's most eager pupil. First contacts with China were mainly through Korea, and many of Korea's borrowings were passed on to Japan after a few years. Confucianism, Chinese script, and Buddhism were seized upon by the Japanese who were early convinced of the superiority of things Chinese. But these by no means end the list, for in due course many other elements of Chinese culture were absorbed, including geomancy, astronomy, music, medicine and ancestor worship. Japan's first great city, Nara, was built on Chinese principles. Some of the Japanese borrowing proved to be inappropriate or unhappy. Thus, early attempts to adopt a Chinese system of land tenure and taxation failed owing to the differences in agricultural conditions and in social structure. Japan remained feudal until the 19th century, while China had cast feudalism aside in the 3rd century BC. Similarly when Japan in the 8th century adopted a bureaucratic system on the Chinese model her attempts to graft this essentially meritocratic system onto her feudal one met with little success. The Japanese, then, absorbed much of Chinese culture, but basic differences in the two societies meant that the original institutions were often greatly altered, and Japan could not always obtain the looked-for improvements from her borrowings. The end of the feudal era in 1868 finally allowed Japan to enter the field of progress, though by that time it was not always the Chinese models that she looked to. Perhaps the greatest legacy of her centuries-long cultural attachment to China now is a linguistic and literary one. Although, like the Koreans, the Japanese ultimately invented their own phonetic script, the Chinese script and the peculiar difficulties of the Chinese language had wrought such havoc on the host language that it has proved impossible even yet to do away with Chinese characters entirely.

Chinese society has had either directly or indirectly, a major influence upon east Asia. It has achieved this through its creation of a seemingly indestructible super-culture which has transcended differences in social structure, custom, language, and historical situation. Such is its power that even the past century and a half of confrontation with western cultures, which in many respects were at least its equals and in economic and military terms certainly its superior, have not destroyed it, though they have modified it. There can be no doubt that the communism of contemporary China is a uniquely Chinese form of communism, a direct heir to much that has gone before, even if inspired by new ideals.

Chinese presence and influence has been so far-reaching that it has not confined itself to the area in this volume.

It has been found, for example, in Mongolia and South-east Asia. Inner Mongolia is now a part of the Chinese People's Republic. And much of South-east Asia has traditionally paid tribute to China, Vietnam having had a relationship with her rather like that of Korea. But there is perhaps no better illustration of the gyroscopic unshakeability of Chinese cultural superiority than that found in the overseas Chinese. Culturally, if not physically, China's influence extends into much of the world.

Chinese settlement overseas has mainly occurred over the last three centuries, usually as a result of population pressure on the southern coasts of China. The most important settlement has been in mainland and island South-east Asia, but there are also large numbers of Chinese in the United States of America, in Canada, in the West Indies, in Britain and many other countries of western Europe. There are two important factors in this movement of Chinese abroad. Almost to a man those who went abroad expected to return to China in due course. They were not truly 'emigrants'. And those who left China were the poorest, least privileged people, people who were forced to leave through economic hardship.

The Overseas Chinese were thus surely the least well-equipped to go beyond the pale of civilization. They were ill-educated men reluctant to leave, and as eager to return, to the only society in the world which was not barbarian. These same men – women rarely left the homeland – carried with them the germ of Chinese superiority. Established overseas they quickly brought into use the powers of organization, hard work, business flair, and sound common sense which had shown to no advantage in their own society. And in many cases they prospered because they were industrious and acute and perhaps because they were able to operate outside the *mores* of whichever host society they were in. Chinese restaurant workers in Britain today, for example, ignore adverse work conditions and long hours which would not be tolerated by native workers, and they grow prosperous on the returns.

The overseas Chinese have always regarded Chinese civilization as the only true one. They have organized themselves along lines which reflect the social organ-ization of their homeland, albeit with adjustments necessary to their peculiar situations overseas. They have created ghettoes (Chinatowns) where they can hug to themselves the illusion that they are in the homeland, and keep away as much as possible from the barbarians amongst whom they dwell. They have left their wives and children in China to keep warm the ancestral home, and they have continued to send money home to them (even while sometimes contracting second marriages in their host country). Before they die they expect to be back in their homeland to be buried in their native soil, but if death comes too soon they will make sure that they are repatriated in their coffins. Even when they are not

first-generation 'emigrants' they still consider themselves Chinese rather than 'foreign'. They look after their own in the face of the barbarians and present a united front to them. They have usually tried to avoid assimilation, setting up enclaves loyal to another state, tending to bleed the economies in which they work by remitting their wealth to China. Not surprisingly the host peoples have looked with suspicion and fear on these aloof and capable representatives of the super-culture. From time to time there have been savage reprisals. And yet, that the overseas Chinese have been generally successful has owed nothing to China's political support. For most of the time of overseas settlement the Chinese government has either refused to acknowledge it (the Ch'ing dynasty did not sanction Chinese leaving their native shores) or has been too weak to attempt support. It was not the might of China which made the Chinese successful, but rather the power of their cultural heritage.

The far east has been dominated by China throughout recorded history. But the concept 'China' implies a sense of national identity which it is perhaps wrong to attribute to the Chinese people. Rather it would be fitting to speak of a sense of cultural identity as the prime feature of Chinese society, and national identity only as a secondary feature stemming from it. It is probable that the majority of villagers of the New Territories of Hong Kong today would consider themselves as Chinese first and British citizens second.

Hence it is possible for China to be defeated, but for the Chinese to be undismayed, for the state to be bankrupt but for the individual Chinese to count themselves wealthy, for the society to be corrupt but for many of its members to be morally strong. It is perhaps from its ancient stock of high culture that the Chinese people is able constantly to renew itself and to maintain its dominance.

The Japanese

An ordered society

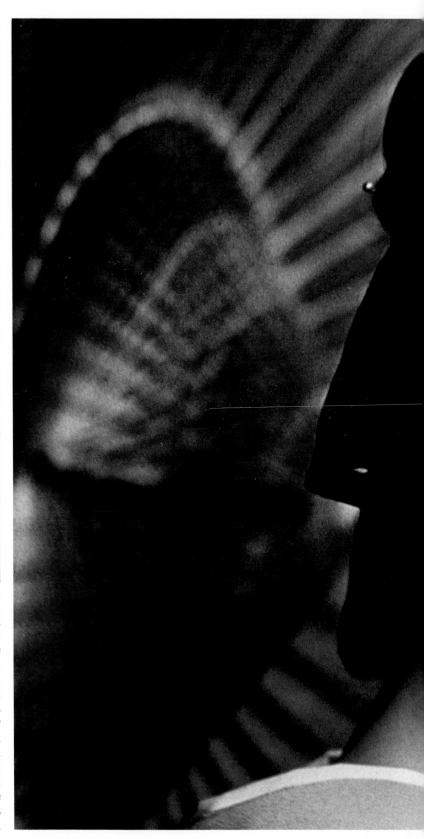

Dressed in sumptuous silk robes the masked actor in a Noh play makes only a few elaborately slow, stylized gestures as he chants the words written centuries before. The stage is very simple. It is floored with the padded rice-straw mats called *tatami* which are used in all ordinary Japanese houses. There is no scenery, only a formalized painting of a pine tree on the back wall, no attempt to create an illusion as in the western theatrical tradition. If it is necessary for an actor to change his costume, a black costumed assistant appears from a tiny 'hurry-door' on to the stage and the actor changes on stage while the music and chanting continue. And yet a dramatic illusion is created. The mask, carved from wood with astounding subtlety, heightens the moods expressed by the changing pace and cadences of the chant. The actor tilts his head forward a fraction, and the mask takes on a look of profound despair. He raises his chin, and a

The women of Japan have not been caught up in the rapid industrial development: they are brought up to be gentle wives and good mothers.

The Japanese

Tokyo was once merely a large provincial town called Edo, but it became a *shogun's* (warlord's) castle town and has grown into a great metropolis.

(Center) Most Japanese have to commute to work, and the railways and subways are always crowded. Special 'pushers' have to be employed.

mysterious joy spreads over the mask.

The traditional forms of art were prepared in an ordered society whose structure was maintained for two hundred years of Japanese isolation from the rest of the world. Japanese traditional society discouraged initiative and individuality and revered the past. The indigenous religion, shinto, was rooted in a sense of awe of natural beauty. Shinto shrines were built in places where the spirits of waterfalls, mountains or trees seemed to have some special power. An ideal of natural beauty marshalled into faultless order lies behind Japanese art.

Japanese art and society share another common basis, in response to lack of resources, in the economic uses of all available material. Japan is a small overcrowded country without natural wealth for her people. In the tea ceremony, in *ikebana* flower arrangement, in the shaping of the tiny *bonsai* trees, and in the gardens of rock and sand, a feeling of space and boundless peace is contained in a miniature form. These ideals are still sought in the crowded, noisy daily life of modern society. Businessmen can be seen at lunchtime choosing stones in the rock department of a large store, and alcoves with a few flowers and a simple hanging scroll provide oases in busy offices. The traditional view of society is that it should be similarly ordered, and a Japanese child learns this from his earliest months.

A baby is carried everywhere by his mother, supported in a sling astride her back. Whenever she bows in greeting, the baby bows with her. He feels her position

Like most other Japanese cities, Tokyo had to be completely rebuilt after suffering severe bomb damage in World War II.

(Right) An almost symmetrical volcanic cone, Fujiyama is, at 12,400 ft., Japan's loftiest mountain. In summer tourists, pilgrims and monks climb it.

The Japanese

in society from her deep bow to a superior, her mere nod to an inferior. As a toddler he is pushed into a bow at appropriate times and learns to use the correct forms of address for the various members of his family and their acquaintances – not for him the simplicity of the one word 'you'. A girl is taught the language forms used by women which reflect their low position.

Until he is six the Japanese child is spoiled and cosseted. But when he is sent off to school he is encouraged to see himself not as an individual but as a representative of his family. His parents will be anxious about his progress, so he needs to be successful to uphold the family prestige. Then the schoolchild learns to identify with a group other than the family. His classmates, his *donen,* will be important to him for the rest of his life, and he charts his progress with reference to them as a standard. Again, although leaders do emerge, the group always takes precedence over the individual, and any unexpected behavior is met with ridicule. Not for nothing do the Japanese use the popular saying: 'The nail that sticks out gets hammered down'. At school much of the child's time is occupied with learning to write. Hard work becomes a habit early on.

The Japanese language, though beautiful and expressive, is in fact a strange and awkward hybrid. Until the 6th century AD there was no written language. Then, with the spread of Buddhism from Korea, the Chinese language was introduced and was used by scholars and priests. Many Chinese words found their way into everyday Japanese and, after unsuccessful attempts to use Chinese characters to represent Japanese phonetically, the language came to be written in a mixed form which persists to this day.

Each Chinese character represents its own meaning, but may be read either as a Japanese word, or pronounced as a Chinese monosyllabic word. Inevitably the pronunciation has changed over the centuries, but the original is often still recognizable. Thus the character 犬 for dog can be read as *'inu'*, the indigenous Japanese word. It can also, when written together with another character, be pronounced *'ken'*, as in 犬歯 *'kenshi'* meaning a canine tooth. But this is not an invariable rule, and 犬小屋 meaning kennel, is pronounced *inugoya.*

Kendo is a traditional Japanese martial art. Before combat begins the Grand Master, Nobuo Higuchi, greets his little pupils.

(Center) Another of the martial arts is Kengeiko, Winter Training, which is mostly exercises in cold sea water at the crack of dawn.

After leaving school or university a well-educated Japanese girl faces harsh discrimination. Apart from a purely academic career, there are very few opportunities for girls and many of them retire to their families rather than accept a dull job. They learn flower arrangement, cooking, music, and wait for a husband. A husband is sometimes found for them through family connections and friends. A certain young man will be mentioned as suitable, his background discussed and his photograph closely examined. If all this seems satisfactory, an *o-miai,* or formal meeting is then arranged at which the parents or a go-between will be present. The formalities usually go no further now, and the young people will continue to meet as they please, and to marry if and when they choose. The wedding ceremony itself may be shinto, Buddhist, or Christian, but whichever it is the bride usually changes two or three times, appearing in traditional formal kimono, in western bridal white, in another elaborate kimono, and finally in ordinary western dress when she leaves the banquet.

The Japanese often seem to reconcile the differences between their traditions and their modern way of life by a similar change of mental dress. The ability to do this may come from the habit of accepting group decisions. As these are in theory unanimous, some members of the group have to come to terms with their own dissent. It is a conflict which leads to a peculiarly Japanese flexibility and ambivalence and has helped them to succeed in a world dominated by the western tradition without entirely abandoning their own. It also means that there is often a noticeable gap between the ideal and the reality in Japan. For all their attention to beauty the Japanese still find it possible to accept the unbearably ugly if it is expedient. Japanese cities are chaotic, sprawling infernos of noise and dirt, with super-highways making hideous ribbons over the crammed buildings. The Japanese similarly finds it possible to maintain the highest standards of behavior in the company of people who know him, but may shove an old lady aside in the rush to get on a crowded train.

Many other aspects of social intercourse are governed by formalities. There is, for example, the precise calculation of the extent of one's indebtedness to others for any help given or favors received. Gifts are exchanged on all possible occasions and these, too, must be of appropriate value. On receiving a gift a Japanese will express his gratitude, accept gracefully, but will refrain from unwrapping it in front of the donor. This ensures that there is no possibility of embarrassment to anyone if it proves unsuitable. And embarrassment, or loss of face, is to be avoided at all costs.

Sumo wrestling champions often top 300 lbs. Contests are brief — the first man to touch the ground, except with his feet, loses the match.

City life

There have been cities in Japan for well over a thousand years, but the story of the modern Japanese city can be taken to begin in the early years of the 17th century when the Tokugawa family seized power from the Imperial court. Establishing their sway over the entire country, the Tokugawas ended a period of prolonged civil war, and created conditions in which cities could grow and prosper.

Tokugawa government took the form of a feudal, hereditary regency. Tokugawa Ieyasu (in Japanese the personal name comes last) and his successors became overlords of all Japan, styling themselves *Shogun* – General, or perhaps Generalissimo. The *daimyo* (nobility), whether they had previously been allies or enemies, were bound to them as vassals. The Emperor had no part in the feudal scheme. During the long rule of the Tokugawas, which lasted from 1603 to 1867, the Emperors were powerless figures, who continued to observe religious and imperial ceremonies in semi-seclusion in Kyoto.

Before the Tokugawa period there had been two great cities in Japan. Kyoto had been, as it was to continue to be, the home of Emperors. Osaka was a commercial town which had become a major political and military center during the civil wars. It lost its political significance after its conquest by the Tokugawa forces in 1615, but because of its geographical position it was important as a great trading city throughout the Tokugawa period, and has grown in modern times into one of the largest cities in the world. Edo, now Tokyo, was merely a large provincial town, but it became the castle town of the *Shogun*.

The *daimyo* had to spend half the year in Edo, half on their own lands. With this system of 'alternate residence' the *Shogun* could keep an eye on his vassals. The upkeep of the *Shogun's* establishments and those of the *daimyo* required the services of hundreds of thousands of people, so that Edo grew from a small settlement in 1600 to a city of a million inhabitants in the middle of the 18th century surpassing Kyoto and Osaka. The distinguishing characteristics of Tokugawa society were hierarchy and

During the autumn celebrations at Nikko, north of Tokyo, men parade dressed as soldiers of the early Tokugawan Shogunate.

(Bottom) A Tokyo musical revue. Over 700 bars and theatres along the Ginza, Tokyo's Times Square, cater to every taste in entertainment.

Japan's young people have adopted the dress and attitudes of the west rather than the traditions of their fathers.

(Right) Kabuki actor Kanzaburo Toshi wearing lion make-up. Kabuki is an ancient and traditional style of acting.

The Japanese

A Japanese farmer rules his own small empire of sons, daughters and their children. But modern city life has eroded ties of filial piety.

The Zen temple at Kyoto is living proof of the ideal of natural beauty marshaled into faultless order which lies behind all Japanese art.

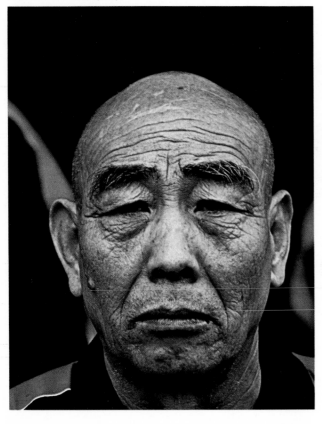

discipline. There were four social classes: warriors (samurai), farmers, craftsmen, and traders, in descending order of precedence. And in normal circumstances it was impossible for a man to move from one class to another. The dress and behavior of each class, and indeed of grades within each class, were carefully defined by the authorities. Whenever the merchants were encouraged by their increasing wealth to assume privileges reserved for the samurai such as carrying swords, 'sumptuary edicts' were issued, renewing the threat of punishment for presumptuousness.

The very layout of the castle town reflected the divisions of society, for within the town there would be separate areas for warriors, craftsmen, and merchants. And in some towns there would even be gates between these areas which would be closed at night. Often the areas themselves would be subdivided into wards, one for each grade of warrior, or for merchants dealing with each type of commodity. Illegal activity was prevented by rigorous administrative devices. Groups of five houses, for example, would be made jointly responsible for the misdemeanors of any one of them.

One of the effects of Tokugawa city administration, then, was to resolve a town into independent parishes which made even city dwellers parochial. As a result, strong feeling for the local community has persisted and 24 it is still considered wise to be well acquainted, if not

Every available inch of land on mountainous Shikoku island is cultivated. The centuries' old pressure on the land is as strong today as ever.

friendly, with one's neighbors. Even today a company may test the suitability of an applicant for a job by surreptitiously asking his neighbor what sort of person he is.

In 1868 the Emperor Meiji was restored to power and the next four decades were devoted to a successful attempt to make up for Japan's late start into the modern world and create a rich and well armed nation. The four classes of society were abolished, and with them restrictions on travel, residence and dress. A new constitution and new laws were passed, and a local and national administration were set up in the European style. Land was made saleable and there were many other reforms and innovations of the economy. Industries were encouraged – especially export industries and those concerned with defense – and railways were built to serve them. Schools and universities were founded, and foreign experts imported to teach them, while Japanese were sent abroad to learn the arts and sciences that would make the country strong.

During the Meiji period (1868-1912) the population of Japan rose by more than half, but the cities grew faster still, so that by 1920 Tokyo contained 3 million people, Osaka nearly 2 million, and Nagoya 600,000, four or five times more than each city had had at the Restoration. Most of this growth was due to industrialization and large numbers of workers were recruited from the countryside to man the factories.

The increase in the population of the cities was not spread evenly over their districts. The centers gained few new inhabitants, while the suburbs grew rapidly with the spread of local railways, which made it possible for people to live in one place and work in another. Under the influence of a peculiarly Japanese form of Confucianism, which included both filial piety and political allegiance to a lord, the government came to conceive of the entire nation as a family, with the Emperor as its head. Therefore the government concerned itself with family organization and household relations, and attempted to preserve in them what was uniquely Japanese. Extensive powers over family members were conferred on household heads, and women became legally incompetent to control property or manage their own affairs. This family form was ill-suited to the needs and habits of those in the lower orders of society; and the problem of maintaining a strict family discipline was particularly great among city dwellers. In the cities there was a tendency for husbands and wives to live independently of the family heads who had legal power over them.

After World War I came a time of economic prosperity, intellectual vitality and political liberalism. It was above all the great cities that set the mood of the age with their universities and mass circulation newspapers. After 1925, when universal male suffrage was introduced, the urban middle classes showed themselves to be firm supporters of socialist, liberal and reform parties.

The cities suffered greatly in World War II. The great metropolises, with the exception of Kyoto, were severely damaged, their flimsy wooden houses far more vulnerable to bombing than the solid buildings of European cities. In single raids tens, and even hundreds of thousands were killed. The lesser industrial centers and the ports and garrison towns – especially, of course, Hiroshima and Nagasaki – were similarly devastated. Normal city life ceased, and the bulk of the city populations moved to the country.

After the defeat, the allied occupation government – in fact run almost entirely by the United States – attempted to reform nearly every feature of social and political life. A new constitution was enacted, establishing parliamentary democracy and stripping the Emperor of all power. Women were given the vote and an education system similar to that of the United States was set up. Certainly the legislation introduced during the occupation helped to alter the form of the Japanese family, especially in the cities. The extended family – dominated by men, if not strictly speaking patrilineal – was abolished, and the new constitution guaranteed equal rights to men and women, and freedom of choice in matters relating to marriage and the family.

Before the war, when the family was considered more important than the feelings of individuals, marriages had usually been arranged for young people by their parents or relatives. Today, though perhaps a quarter of all marriages are arranged, this usually means only that suitable partners are introduced to each other, so that they themselves can decide whether or not to marry. On the other hand, in contracting 'love marriages' Japanese people often show a peculiarly hard-headed approach to romance. Most girls now work after leaving school or college and often marry young men they meet at the office. Both men and women tend to give great weight to practical considerations: men look for health in their future wives, while women pay attention to the earning power or potential of their suitors.

The typical city family today consists of husband, wife and one or two children – couples are having fewer children than before – living in a small flat or perhaps a suburban house. Within the family there will be an almost complete division of labor. The husband will only have time for family affairs on Sunday, for working hours are long, and commuting distances very great. Any entertainment of business associates takes place in bars and restaurants after working hours for guests are very seldom invited home. His wife, who will be ill-acquainted with the details of her husband's job, will herself have stopped work before, or soon after marrying. Few women aspire to careers, and those who do find employers most reluctant to treat women, and especially older women, on anything like equal terms with men. The wife looks after the household finances, and many 25 husbands offer their wives their entire pay packets, receiving in return their allowance for tobacco and bars. The wife will also concern herself with the children's education. The education system is fiercely competitive and mothers – 'education mothers' as they are called – frequently go to great lengths to have their children coached, or arrange other advantages over their rivals at school. Finally the wife handles relations with the local community on behalf of the whole family; the husband, away most of the time, will know as little of the neighbors as she will of his colleagues at work.

Because so many young couples prefer to live apart from their parents, older people are no longer able to depend on the support of their children when they stop work – a state of affairs morally disturbing to those generations brought up under the old family system, with its Confucian emphasis on filial piety. The rapid increase in life expectancy after the war, the meagerness of state pensions and the fact that few employers offer pensions at all, have combined to make the care of the old one of the most serious of many social problems afflicting Japan, and in particular the cities.

Though the family has changed its form, and though it is now less common for more than two generations to live together, kinship relations continue to be extremely important in Japanese social life. It would have been difficult, for example, for the cities to grow as fast as they have done since the war, and with so little disruption (in spite of the lack of social services), if immigrants to the cities – often younger sons of farmers – had not been able to depend on their relations to look after them temporarily and find them jobs.

Another important change in city society in the postwar period, this time one in which the occupation authorities were not directly concerned, involved employment and the labor market. In the early years of Japanese industrialization workers had moved frequently from employer to employer. In order to reduce this labor mobility firms were forced to offer their workers better terms and a variety of welfare benefits such as free housing. Virtue was made of necessity by idealizing paternalism. In Japanese companies, unlike those elsewhere, employers of all types would work together like a family.

After the war jobs were scarce. It became customary for workers to join companies straight from school, and to stay with them indefinitely, since it was not easy to change jobs for the better. In large companies employment seemed to be for life, and employees received all sorts of rewards, besides their pay, almost without regard to their abilities or contributions to the company. Wages rose according to age and length of service, so that older men, though they might be less efficient than young ones, received far more money for doing the same jobs, and so were easily able to meet their family commitments.

26

Fishermen stand under gray winter skies. Fish, rice and a huge variety of vegetables form the basic Japanese diet.

(Bottom) Many farmers commute to the city during the week leaving their wives and daughters to tend the farm until the weekend.

(Right) The antithesis of the frail and flowerlike geisha, fisherwomen in Hokkaido will take the boat out themselves if their men fall sick.

The Japanese

Furnaces in Yawata produce
red-hot molten steel to feed
Japan's flourishing
ship-building and motor
manufacturing industries.

28

Recently there have been fewer teenagers ready to enter the labor market, and so it has become increasingly difficult for companies to pay employees more as they grow older. It is possible that the shortage of young people in the labor market may alter the organization of industrial companies and the social relations within them. Perhaps no post-war development indicated the intellectual and spiritual turmoil of the cities better than the new religions flourishing in them.

Typically these religions, which have certain obvious resemblances to messianic cults in other parts of the world, were founded by individuals who claim to have been suddenly enlightened or divinely possessed. The religious teachings are usually simple; and their promise is as often of success, including material success, in this world, as of spiritual satisfaction or a better life to come. Many of the religions concern themselves with faith healing. Their organizations, commonly presided over by disciples of the founder, usually allow their members to participate extensively in the rites and practices of the faith. The appeal of the new religions has been greatest among those people who have gained least from the changes that have taken place since the war – old people, women living alone in the big cities, or workers in declining industries.

Japan has today become a nation of cities. More than half the population lives along the coastal strip extending from Kobe in the west to Chiba in the east and there are forecasts of even faster forms of transport than the present extremely rapid trains which could cause the separate cities of the region to be fused into one vast settlement. The problems of the city have become those of all Japan in spite of the relatively high proportion of people still working on the land.

It is not easy to predict how Japanese cities will fare in the future, but one important development is the increasing concern of people, and consequently governments, for public works and welfare. For all their present wealth Japanese cities have grown too fast for their own good, without enough parks and libraries, drains, roads and underground railways. It now seems likely that more money will be spent on these and the cities will become pleasanter to live in. With the growth of foreign trade and involvement in world affairs the larger cities will become more international in quality. At present Tokyo and Osaka, despite their enormous populations, are far from cosmopolitan and few of their inhabitants have had any kind of dealings with foreigners, except those foreigners who, like Koreans, were once Japanese subjects.

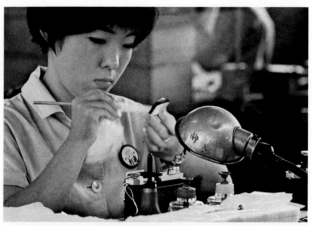

Japanese girls are famous for their ability to work with care and precision on the most delicate equipment – like this girl assembling a Nikon camera.

(Bottom) Workers take a break while working on the 40-mile long Seikan tunnel connecting Hokkaido and the main island of Honshu.

Country life

The Japanese believe bathing refreshes the spirit even more than the body. The mud baths at Beppu are believed to cure many ailments as well.

One of the most striking features of Japanese rural society is its uniformity. Although many regional dialects exist in Japan, differences in speech are not usually great enough seriously to hinder communications between people from separate regions of the country. In this respect Japan differs markedly from India and China. Differences in the rural way of life from one part of Japan to another are even less pronounced than those of speech, and at first are barely perceptible to the foreign observer. Most villages and hamlets throughout the country appear at first glance to be virtually identical and regional peculiarities in buildings and layout can only be identified by a practised eye.

The hamlet, with its tightly-clustered group of farmhouses and shops, is the characteristic form of rural settlement throughout Japan. Isolated farmhouses are found only in a few mountain and upland districts. Today the typical hamlet remains small and consists of about 40 farm households and 25 non-farm households which own shops or provide other services.

Recent economic growth has brought unprecedented prosperity to the hamlets of Japan, and has given rise to some startling incongruities. Television aerials sprout from the thatched roofs of farmhouses, whose low-ceilinged kitchens gleam with an array of modern household appliances, ranging from electric rice-cookers to automatic washing machines. The roar of motorcycles and farm trucks shakes the village streets, where until recently the bicycle represented the most modern form

30

Few women wear kimonos now, but for special occasions like the autumn celebrations in Nikko, many of the older women put on their finery.

(Center) Dressed in traditional splendor for her Shinto wedding, a bride begins her married life as the lowest person in the household.

of transport. Nevertheless many traditional aspects of Japanese rural life have survived.

There can be no doubt that the overwhelming importance of the rice crop since very early times helps to explain the strong community spirit of the Japanese hamlet. In paddy rice cultivation, the freedom of the farmer to act as an individual is severely restricted by the need to irrigate the terraced fields which demands the co-operation of all the farmers in the neighborhood. So it is hardly surprising that in Japanese rural society the community is regarded as being far more important than the individual. Indeed, throughout Japanese society as a whole, a very high value is attached to co-operation and consensus; individual initiative is often frowned upon.

Despite land reform and other more recent changes, the average Japanese farm remains small. Most holdings consist of a mere 2·5 acres of arable land. This small size is largely a result of extreme land scarcity. Japan is a small, mountainous country. Only 16 per cent of its entire surface is cultivable. Yet the population, now over 104 million, is currently the seventh largest in the world. The pressure of population on very limited land resources has been felt for centuries and has given rise to a remarkable intensity of land use. Until very recently, for instance, practically every square yard of cultivable land has been devoted to some sort of crop production.

As well as being very small, the average holding is fragmented into widely scattered strips and parcels of land. This, and also the absence of enclosure, accentuate the need for farmers to work co-operatively.

While many features of rural life in Japan have remained essentially unchanged for centuries, modernization and the emergence of Japan as one of the world's leading industrial nations has inevitably brought about radical changes in the countryside. These began in the late 19th century when Japan's long isolation from the rest of the world ended. Among the innovations imported from western countries and adapted to Japanese conditions were many which greatly affected the farmer. One of these, for instance, was the use of chemical fertilizers, which proved to be far more effective in raising yields than the traditional equivalents. At the same time the growth of large industrial cities started an exodus of labor from the land. This rural-urban migration, however, did not lead to depopulation of the countryside, partly because, in the Japanese family system, the entire estate was inherited by the eldest son. This meant that in the typical Japanese farm family the eldest son remained on the farm, leaving the younger sons and daughters free to migrate to the cities in search of factory employment.

These changes during the latter half of the 19th century were accompanied by a rapid increase in tenancy until by 1900 nearly half the arable land was tilled by tenant farmers. Another important development was the introduction in 1872 of compulsory education, which soon

Japanese homes are private and guests rarely entertained in the home. Sharing a large communal bath, however, is a popular form of relaxation.

(Bottom) Parents of dead children decorate and worship the Buddha of the Children in the Sanjusangende Temple in Kyoto.

produced an almost fully literate rural society. Yet on the eve of World War II hamlet life, particularly in the outlying regions of the country, retained much of its traditional character, and in a surprising number of respects was much the same as it had been for two or three centuries. Rice, then as now, was of far greater importance than any other cereal, and by far the greatest proportion of time spent in the fields was devoted to its cultivation. Boiled rice formed the staple diet of the villagers, and liquor was also derived from rice. Rice was often also used as a form of money.

In many villages silk came second to rice as a source of income, supplying the western market. The depression of the 1930s and the collapse of the market for silk brought widespread poverty to the farmers.

Some farm households possessed a cow or a horse, not for milk or meat but as a draft animal. The average diet was generally overwhelmingly vegetarian and the main source of animal protein was fish rather than meat. Wherever possible a wide variety of fruit and vegetables was cultivated, usually for local consumption.

The tools and agricultural implements used by farm families were mainly simple and often rather primitive and the few petrol engines used to drive threshing and rice hauling machines were owned either by the local 31

(Over page) Clad in loincloths, 8,000 youths scramble for a lucky stick thrown in their midst by a priest during the winter festival in Okinawa.

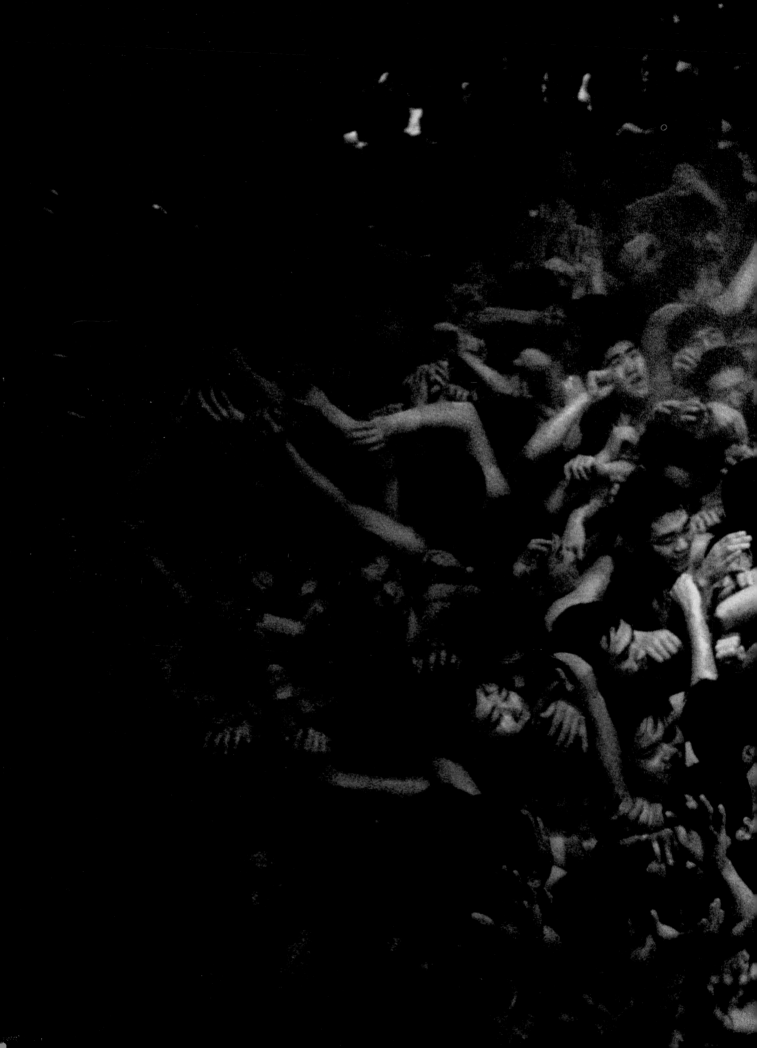

The Japanese

For all their wealth cities have grown too fast — busy, crowded and sprawling — but a few quiet corners remain near temples and shrines.

(Center) In the 6th century Japan was overwhelmed by disasters. The *Aoi Matsuri* or Hollyhock Festival gives thanks for a safe deliverance.

(Right) A line of student tourists ascends the slopes of volcanic Mount Aso, smaller than the revered Mount Fujiyama.

Agricultural Co-operative Society or by a few wealthy farmers. Machinery was little used in the fields, and the laborious tasks of tilling, planting, weeding and harvesting were all done by hand. Indeed, the intensive use of human labor was the outstanding feature of pre-war Japanese agriculture.

Then the basic unit of hamlet life was the household, which was invariably organized around a descent line of males. Headship of the family, and the family estate, was inherited by the eldest son and passed on in turn to *his* eldest son, and so on. The aim of the Japanese family system was to ensure the indefinite perpetuation of the family line. Such was the importance of securing a male heir to continue the family line that if there were no sons, the husband of one of the daughters would be adopted into the family.

Status in the household was determined by age and sex. The youngest son was required to be strictly obedient to the eldest son, and to his father and grandfather. Daughters occupied a far lower place in the family hierarchy and were expected to be subservient to all the male members of the household. New families would sometimes be established as branches of existing ones, usually when the size and resources of the family were sufficiently plentiful. Then a second son would be given enough land and property to function as the head of his own household and establish a new line of descent. This new household would be known as the *bunke* to differentiate it from the main household, which was known as the *honke*. Relations between the *honke* and *bunke* tended to remain hierarchical. The *bunke* acknowledged the authority of the *honke*.

In poorer areas of the country, where physical environments were harsh and where there was a particularly strong need for households to co-operate, larger groupings known as *dozoku* would develop. *Dozoku* would often include households which were not related as well as the *honke* and *bunke*. These non-related households — which often originated when land was granted by a senior household to one of its servants or retainers — formed the lowest stratum in the *dozoku* hierarchy. They were dependent on and subservient to the senior household of the *dozoku*. The senior family of the *dozoku* group commonly owned most of the arable land. The non-related families in the group held only token portions of land. As these were generally not enough to support them in effect they became tenants working on the land of the senior family and a conspicuously master-servant relationship developed between landlord and tenant. The landlord paternalistically undertook to support his tenants, particularly during times of crop failure, while the tenants were expected to serve him in return in and around his farmhouse, and to show him due respect and loyalty at all times.

The head of the Japanese farm household enjoyed a position of great authority. The eldest son also had high

34

Each winter 4 million visitors invade sparsely populated Hokkaido to see huge sculptures of ice and snow in the February Snow Festival.

The Japanese

Cages containing oysters are suspended from rafts at Tobe Bay. Three times a year the cages are lifted and the rate of pearl growth is checked.

(Center) Women divers, *ama*, are trained from childhood to stay under water for over a minute collecting oysters in their wooden buckets.

A pearl 'doctor' inserts a nucleus into a healthy oyster. Countless layers of mother of pearl laid over the nucleus will form the pearl itself.

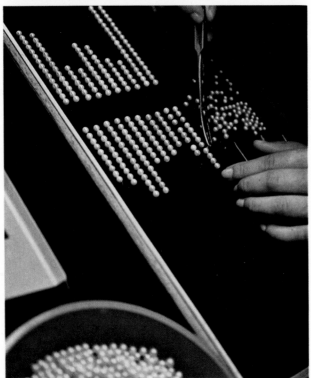

On Mikimoto Island, center of the industry, pearls are classified by color and size. Pink is the best color, then white, yellow and black.

status. Women were regarded as far less important. Most families welcomed the birth of a single daughter, who could assist with the running of the household and with the upbringing of the younger children but the birth of too many daughters was regarded as little short of disastrous, since a dowry had to be provided for each of them. Marriages were hardly ever made on the basis of love and affection between the two partners, but were arranged by the heads of the two households which were to be united. This arrangement is still surprisingly common in Japanese villages today. When the daughter married she became entirely subordinate not only to her husband but also to her husband's family. She was expected to show obedience at all times to her mother-in-law. The bride, in fact, occupied the most lowly status in the household. She was the first to rise in the morning and the last to retire at night. She was expected to provide meals, look after the children and work alongside the men in the fields. Only when she became a mother-in-law could she begin to enjoy any sort of authority in the household.

The defeat of Japan in 1945 and the new democratic constitution provided a basis for radical changes in Japanese society. Dramatic economic growth since 1955 has resulted in an extraordinary rise in the standard of living of the Japanese, city dwellers and farmers alike.

Perhaps the most far-reaching development of the immediate post-war years in rural society was land reform. In 1946 under this reform the Japanese government began to purchase the lands of all absentee landlords, together with those portions of tenanted land larger than one hectare (four hectares in Hokkaido) and transferred these to their former tenants on a deferred payment basis. Japan was transformed almost overnight from a nation of tenant farmers into a nation of owner-occupiers. The farmer was relieved of the need to pay rents which often amounted to half his income and began to enjoy unprecedented prosperity. And the power of the landlord in the village community was greatly diminished. The master-servant relationship associated with the pre-war tenancy system virtually disappeared.

The provisions of the post-war constitution gradually began to modify other relationships in the village and in the farm family. Pre-war legislation had stressed the virtues of authoritarianism and of community discipline. The new constitution guaranteed the rights of the individual. These democratic and egalitarian reforms have inevitably contributed to the gradual weakening of hierarchies in the household and in the community.

But perhaps the most powerful agent of change in rural society since 1945 has been the development of Japan's industrial economy. This has resulted in a variety of technological innovations which have helped to transform Japanese agriculture. One such innovation has been the small and inexpensive hand tractor, driven by a petrol engine and ideally suited to the minute fields of the typical Japanese farm. Equipped with a hand tractor, the Japanese farmer can plow and harrow his fields in a fraction of the time needed when only draft animals were used. The wide range of chemical weedkillers now available has eliminated the time-consuming and laborious task of weeding by hand and improved types of fertilizer and insecticide have greatly improved the crops.

In rice cultivation, which remains the mainstay of Japanese agriculture, cold-resistant strains of rice have been developed. And vinyl sheets used to protect seedlings have also helped to raise the rice output.

Dietary changes, too, have had their effect. Westernization of the Japanese diet, partly as a result of American occupation and partly owing to increasing prosperity, has brought increased demand for items like milk and butter. Livestock products, which were of negligible importance before 1945, now contribute almost a fifth of the total value of Japanese agricultural output. Fruit and vegetables market gardening has also grown in importance.

The rice subsidy provided by the Japanese government has also played its part in increasing prosperity in the countryside. After World War II the government retained its control over the collection and distribution of rice and paid the farmer an agreed price for his saleable crop. During the 1960s the government regularly raised this agreed price to the considerable benefit of the farmer but to the dismay of the urban consumer. Ostensibly, the aim of this policy was to eliminate the gap between rural and urban incomes, but in reality the rice subsidy was used by the ruling Liberal Democratic Party as a means of retaining the rural vote. This policy not only brought about a large rice surplus, but also further raised the income of the farmer, who by 1970 enjoyed virtually the same standard of living as the city dweller.

Farmers have meanwhile become increasingly involved in part-time work in factories. Indeed by 1970 half of the income of the average Japanese farm household was derived from employment outside agriculture. In farming districts in the hinterlands of Tokyo, Osaka and Nagoya for instance, it is usual for the male members of the farm family to commute on weekdays to work in factories leaving the farm under supervision of the farmer's wife and the retired grandparents. At the weekend, the farmer and his sons return to undertake the heavier farming tasks.

The growth of employment opportunities in the cities has also caused heavy population migration from the outlying regions of the country. Isolated rural districts are beginning to suffer from depopulation, particularly the loss of younger people.

All these post-war changes have combined to transform relationships within the family. With so many opportunities for employment outside agriculture, eldest sons do not always want to inherit the farm, and a growing number of them prefer to sever their links with the land and establish their own homes in the cities. Another changing role is that of the farmer's wife who enjoys a far higher status in the family now that she is entrusted for so much of the time with the management of the farm. Meanwhile, many daughters commute to jobs in city offices, shops, and factories, and the majority of them are increasingly unwilling to marry into farm households.

Yet it is unlikely that a massive exodus from the countryside will lead to a sharp fall in the number of farm households. Despite the fact that the total population living in farm households continues to fall, the total number of households shows a far slower rate of decline. This is partly due to extreme land shortage and scarcity of housing in the cities, a factor which discourages many farmers from abandoning their holdings.

As time goes on, the distinction between the way of life of the Japanese city-dweller and that of the farmer becomes increasingly blurred. Almost all farm households own a television set, an electric washing machine and a refrigerator and many Japanese farmers are now able to take holidays abroad. In view of this remarkable prosperity, it is surely no longer appropriate to think of the Japanese farmer as a 'peasant' even though many aspects of his way of life may be derived from the peasant society of pre-modern Japan.

Ainu
Japan

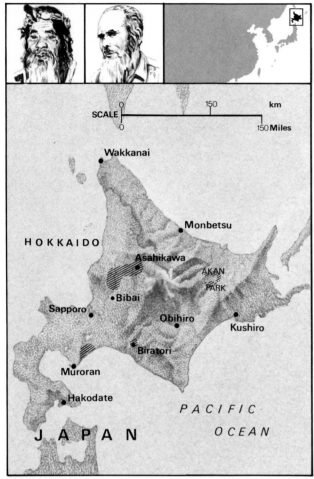

The Ainu are a vanishing race. Even in their main habitat, Hokkaido – the northernmost of the large Japanese islands – these individual people, who were once so clearly different from their neighbors, are fast becoming absorbed into the now dominant Japanese population. In 1970 there were thought to be 16,000 Ainu on Hokkaido of whom only about one per cent were of pure blood. Some live on Sakhalin under the Russian régime and it is thought that a few survive on the Asian mainland, on the Kuril islands and on the Kamchatka peninsula.

Hairiness is the Ainu's outstanding physical characteristic. Ainu hairiness extends all over their bodies and is distinguished by the thickness and length of each of their individual hairs. The Ainu are often called 'the hairy Ainu'. Ainu men grow beautiful beards and moustaches. Their eyes lack the mongol fold and their irises are often chestnut. Their noses are prominent. In fact the Ainu look quite different to the Japanese and other mongoloid peoples who surround them. Osteologically they are nearer to the Maori. They have one of the world's greatest ratios of trunk to leg (sitting height).

Sapporo, the main town of Hokkaido, lies at a lati-

Fewer than 300 full-blooded
Ainu remain in Hokkaido;
their unique tradition
is fully exploited as a
tourist attraction.

Ainu Japan

(Below) The Ainu no longer inhabit these huts of wood and straw. They are kept in the village for the sake of curious Japanese tourists.

Ainu women have their lips tattooed blue at seventeen. This shows their eligibility and protects the mouth from being entered by evil spirits.

tude of 43°N. The climate is similar to that of the north-east coastal region of the USA on the same latitude except that the snowfall here is much heavier. Unlike the rest of Japan, Hokkaido does not have high humidity in summer.

The Ainu of Hokkaido lived virtually undisturbed by the Japanese until the 17th century. It was not until the end of the 19th century that colonists began to convert their land into the arable and pastoral farms that cover much of it today. During the 19th century the Ainu, especially those nearest Japan, gradually learnt about agriculture. As their contact with the Japanese increased they came more and more to practise primitive agriculture, using wooden implements to grow hardy cereals, edible roots, plants and fruit. Shellfish remained a significant part of their diet. They worked no metals, but acquired iron tools and weapons from traders. They made no pottery. Their equipment was usually wooden.

The Ainu are skilled carvers. Some of their tools and weapons are decorated, such as the carved wooden scabbards that sheath their famous swords. These may be family treasures, originating from Japan or the Asian continent. One hears of the use of swords in the *yukar* or Ainu epic, which has long descriptions of battles, possibly referring to the fierce resistance the Ainu of north Japan put up to their expulsion around 1,000 AD.

The Ainu version of the cradle: the baby is suspended from a bamboo *shunta,* where it can be rocked and lulled to sleep.

(Below) The bear cult is rooted in Ainu tradition. This fearsome skull, held in a forked stick, forms part of an altar in Nibutani.

The Ainu's fundamental way of life centered on hunting, fishing and gathering. The surrounding seas and rivers were – and still are – full of fish. In the interior are bears, deer and other game. Seal and even whales provided the Ainu with good food. They hunted with spears, fish-traps, bows and arrows all made from available materials like antlers, wood, vegetable bindings and so on. Deer, which they killed with the help of dogs, provided most of their meat, while salmon was their second most abundant food. Caught in traps or speared, the salmon were carefully dissected, and their flesh dried. Great care was taken in handling the flesh and the various parts of the fish were given specific names, in a way similar to that by which Europeans identify the different parts of a carcass of beef.

The bear was the only animal in Ainuland that was able to fight back to the extent of killing its hunter. Great care was taken in hunting expeditions. If, for example, a bear was discovered holed up in its den, a bow and poisoned arrow would be set up so that it could be triggered off at a distance by a cord, to shoot the bear when it emerged. The same device might be set up along a bear's favorite route.

One of the fundamental notions of Ainu religious beliefs was that all living beings and natural phenomena were *kamui,* a word remarkably like the Japanese word *kami* used for something like a god in *shinto,* the native religion. Individual animals were treated as *kamui,* and also were thought of as part of the wider *kamui* that was the guardian and essence of the whole species. When, in spring, as the snow was melting, the Ainu prepared to hunt the bears the call of the owl announced the hunting season of the bear – the *kamui* of the mountains. The hunt took place in an area usually thought to be the special preserve of the family of the hunter, although an area in which a member of the family had previously been wounded by the bear would be scrupulously avoided. It was thought that the bears that lived there had some special grudge against the family. Great attention was paid to dreams during the expedition and if they were of ill omen, the party would abandon the chase. If a stream had to be crossed, special prayers were addressed to the *kamui* of the stream and *inau,* representing gods, were erected. *Inau* are wands of willow or some other wood, from which shavings are half removed, making a mass of fringes in a possibly infinite variety of patterns. The top of the wand is decorated or shaped to symbolize the god which the *inau* represents. On reaching the bear's den the hunters would greet it just as if they were visiting the home of a human being. They would invite it back to their own home for entertainment. Sometimes they blocked the entrance with logs, to hamper the bear's escape.

The Ainu are famous for their bear cult. In the spring they captured bear cubs and brought them back to the village to be reared. As tiny cubs they were kept in the **41**

Ainu Japan

In a workshop for carvers an Ainu artist produces animal figures from the local softwood. A particular favorite is the bear.

(Below) In the Saru valley an Ainu woman weeds rice seedlings. From these come their basic food, and *sake* – rice wine.

To treat a crippled man praying women tie his limbs with bullrush stems and beat him gently. This should banish the evil spirits away.

With no written language Ainu transmit their history and teachings in song and dance. This occasion is the opening of the tourist village.

home and brought up with the children, often sharing the mother's milk with her baby. Everything was done to make a bear cub happy. When it was too large to be kept in the house it was moved to a wooden cage. It would still be treated lovingly and indeed respectfully, because the Ainu believed it had been entrusted to them by the gods. It was fed well, talked to and given pieces of wood to play with. This treatment might last for as long as three years. Eventually the bear-cub was ceremonially dispatched to join its dead parents.

The time for sending young bears home was winter, before the new hunting season. *Inau* were made, rice wine brewed and decorated arrows and cakes made ready. On the appointed day the bear was removed from its cage and tethered. Decorated arrows were shot at it. These irritated the bear and its movements were interpreted as a dance of joy at its impending journey. Then a man would shoot a hunting arrow into its heart, and its neck was pressed between two logs to make sure it was dead. Its head was set amidst the gifts of cakes and the other delicacies given to it to take as presents to its dead parents. It was entreated to tell its parents how well it had been cared for, so that the village might continue to receive favors. In many villages the bear's skull finished up on a stake, with many others, in a sort of sacred hedge or enclosure.

Most Ainu gods are represented by differently patterned *inau* set up in rows outside houses or elsewhere to be worshipped and to receive offerings. Certain Ainu men may be asked to help in times of trouble and can transmit prayers when a favor is required from the gods. Some women, too, can help, for they can be visited or possessed by gods, they can heal or fortell the future. In fact their women had many of the attributes of shamans and some may have used the typical Siberian equipment of cap and drum. The preponderance of females as shamans in Hokkaido conforms to the Japanese pattern, where shamans also tend to be women.

An Ainu house is traditionally built of roughly trimmed logs bound together into a frame of four walls. Its roof had sloping gables. The gaps between the logs are filled with thatch of twigs or bamboo grass. They are built in villages often facing east. In front of the house is the god-window, by which *kamui* could come and go. Men enter through a door on the west side. In the center of the floor is a rectangular hearth, the smoke from which emerges through holes in the roof. A cooking pot hangs on a hook of adjustable height. The family possessions are hung on the timbers or stored in the ceiling. In former days a well-off family would have a fair amount of equipment, including Japanese articles, such as decorated swords, silk kimonos and, more recently, china bowls and all sorts of household gear.

For winter clothing the Ainu used any furs and skins they had managed to lay their hands on. Footwear was made from fish-skins. For summer and ceremonial wear they used bark fiber from various trees such as elms and lindens. These fibers were woven on simple looms into cloth which sometimes incorporated all-over patterns to which appliqué designs in white, red and other colors were added. The garments which they made with this cloth resembled the Japanese style, but the Ainu also made their own style of caps and hoods.

Ainu women's girdles were kept secret from men. Every Ainu woman made her own secret girdle from a pattern taught her by either her mother or some other female relative. Although in other respects the Ainu are patrilineal, girdle patterns, it seems, were hereditary through the mother's line. Waving these girdles in the air was a powerful charm against all evil influences.

Women made themselves look beautiful by tattooing: the detail of the design differed from one region to another, but tended basically to be a pattern round the lips, usually with pointed ends which looked like a flourishing moustache. Wavy lines were drawn across their eyebrows and lower arms: the backs of their hands and their fingers were decorated with diamond patterns and rings. All this tattooing was normally completed by the age of 17 or 18. As the woman grew older the tattooing faded. Descriptions of old Ainu women sometimes refer to their barely visible tattooing, a sign of their past beauty. Men, who were not usually tattooed for decoration, were sometimes tattooed as a treatment for illness.

Ainu men marry only one partner. Couples usually live away from their parents in their own house. Ainu children are beguiled with songs and games. Adults, too, enjoy drinking, dancing and singing, telling tales of animal *kamui* or legends of the greater gods, culminating in the great epics of love and war. Traditionally men would recite these epics lying in a drunken semi-trance on the floor. They chanted out the old tales, thumping their chests with each hand alternately while the audience beat out the rhythm with pieces of wood. One such piece of wood was the decorated 'moustache-lifter' or libation wand, a typically male Ainu possession which they held across the top of a wine-cup to hold up the moustache when they drank.

Ainu also assembled together to decide on the guilt of an alleged wrongdoer and impose penalties. The village head, after consultation with the council of elders, pronounced judgement. The culprit might have his ear or nose removed. Or he might be sentenced to exile, or to a buffeting with heavy knobbed and ringed clubs. The death penalty was never given.

Just enough is left and just enough has been recorded of Ainu culture to give an insight into a very individual way of life which survived from the very distant past to the very near present. It is enough to give one a notion of the mentality of a hunting people who not only loved and were completely involved in the environment which sustained them, but had a sentimental relationship with the animals it had to kill in order to live.

43

Aborigines of Taiwan

44

Paiwan women of the third
largest tribe of Taiwan
aborigines don beautifully
decorated clothes to
attend a village wedding.

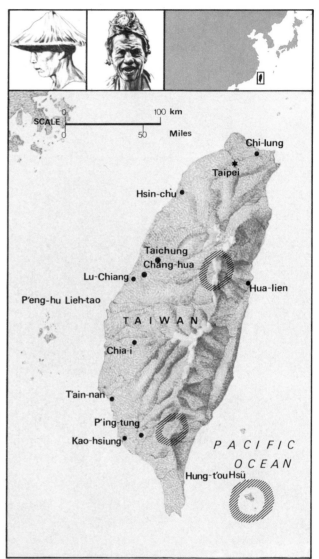

Tribal legends are usually transmitted to the rest of the world by outsiders, but a member of the Tsou tribe of Taiwan aborigines, Moqo Muknana, has himself told the story of his people's origins and present way of life.

'When the world was flooded' Muknana begins 'peoples assembled on Mount Jade (13,000 feet, the highest mountain on the island) . . . When the world was no longer flooded peoples scattered and lived in all directions separately. They looked for land to be fields. They discussed and said "My land is here. We shall not rob each other." There came out the man they would listen to. There came out the headman. It began at that time . . .

'They heard someone cutting with an axe. They said to their ears "What is like this?" It turned out that it was Chinese who came from the opposite side of the 45

sea. The Chinese were afraid of the Tsou. They showed a pot to the Tsou. The Tsou liked the pot very much. They showed the axe. They showed the sword. The Tsou said "Very good things! We shall be friendly with the Chinese." The Tsou admired the people of the plain. They intended to imitate . . .

'Nowadays the Tsou have altered their old ways. We admire those who send their children to school. Compare the ancient way of doing things with that of the present. We have changed. We shall work even more vigorously. We shall imitate the way of doing things we have seen on the plain. We admire people whose livelihood is so good. We shall send our children to school. We shall know more and the other people will not cheat us.' As the legend shows Taiwan's aborigines profess eagerness to adopt new ways and be assimilated into the mainstream of Taiwan society.

Taiwan, called Formosa, the beautiful isle, by the Portuguese, is a small island half the size of Ireland. Against Ireland's 3 million population it contains a 16 million population, which is increasing fast. Most now live on the western plain. In two-thirds of the island it is mountainous and cultivation is difficult.

The first mainland settlers came and settled in numbers in Taiwan about half a millennium ago either absorbing

(Top) For centuries Taiwan aborigines were naturally isolated on the misty mountain tops. Today visitors need special passes to enter their territories.

The wedding feast provides an occasion for members of many villages to assemble in Ma-Chia and enjoy the food and the gaiety

The Paiwan are skilled in embroidery and beadwork. The main motifs are human figures and snakes which have a legendary significance.

Chinese immigrants, the aboriginal peoples of Taiwan have throughout retained their identity. More than two hundred thousand of these people, just 2 per cent of the total population, survive in the mountain forests today. Culturally and linguistically the tribes belong to the Malayo-Polynesian group of peoples. All except the traditionally peaceable Yami were, until the practice was prohibited under the island's period of Japanese rule from 1895 to 1945, warlike headhunting peoples.

Higher up the mountains than any other aboriginal tribe live the Bunun. They carve picture calendars on boards, reckoning the months by changes in the moon. Like both the Atayal and the Tsou they extract men and women's back teeth. Otherwise, it is felt, people's jaws are similar to dogs and monkeys. Their tribal land is divided between clan groups into hunting territory. Hunting is more important than anything else to the Bunun and their lives, like most hunting peoples, are bound up with their prey. Most of their stories tell of humans transformed into animals, of sexual relations between humans and animals and of the metamorphoses of animals into humans. The 'shooting the beast's ear ceremony' is their most important festival. This is when, in mid-summer, all babies under one year old are carried to the village house in which ears of deer, roebuck, goats and wild boar are hung on a board. On behalf of each baby an adult shoots at these from six feet. If his arrow hits the target the baby will be a good hunter. If he fails the baby will probably soon die.

The Atayal, too, live high in the mountains. Like all the other tribes on the island they are slash-and-burn cultivators, but they are the only group of Taiwan aborigines who have no pottery nor any memory of having had it in the past. All the things they use are made of wood, gourd, bamboo and rattan. They are famous for their weaving and for their beaded skirts. All the men and women tattoo their foreheads, but only headhunters can tattoo their chins, and only the women who are skilful weavers may tattoo their cheeks. The Atayal replace clan groups with ritual groups called *gaga*. A *gaga* is made up of a core of close relatives and friends headed by a chief who, together with the other *gaga* chiefs, holds the informal political authority of the settlement. The *gaga* in fact must satisfy all the rules and demands made by *utux* – all the supernatural beings of all kinds, including ancestral spirits, ghosts and gods – for any violation of tradition angers the *utux* and pollutes and endangers the community.

The Ami, who live along most of the east coast and in the valley between the central and coastal mountains, are the largest group of Taiwan aborigines. Many of their settled, densely populated villages house over a thousand people. Their society is matrilineal and where a man lives and the terms of his inheritance and succession are determined by his mother's clan. Women, however, are excluded from village politics. Their politi-

the aboriginal population of the plains or driving them into the mountains. Far from the cultural center in Peking the dominant Chinese community developed its own splinter island ways and dialect. For half a century Taiwan was a Japanese province, almost forgotten by mainland China. Then came the next convulsing influx.

As Mao Tse-tung's victorious army made its last sweep into south-eastern China in 1949 no less than two million people, loyal to the Republican ideal of Chiang Kai-shek and knowing that surrender could easily end in execution, embarked frantically for what to them was the unknown distant Chinese island of Taiwan. Into a quiet peasant population of Han stock with their own deeply rooted Taiwanese personality, there thus descended in relatively enormous numbers army officers and merchants, government officials, members of parliament and business executives. The newcomers saw themselves as a dispossessed élite. They fretted for their return to the mainland, and even continued the charade of legislating for the mainland country over which they had lost all power. Beneath the two layers of population of mainland origin there remained the remnants of the aboriginal population. Among the natural fortifications of Taiwan's mountainous interior, traditionally shunned by the

47

The snake motif recalls that noble ancestors emerged from eggs bitten by a great spirit snake and commoners' ancestors from the eggs of a green snake.

The women of Ma-Chia prepare the wedding feast. The guests will soon enjoy their biscuits and succulent pork dishes.

cal organization is based on age-grades. In the village the men's house serves as a dormitory, a military barracks and a ritual center which a boy enters at 15.

For the next four or five years the boy prepares himself by undergoing various kinds of physical training and instruction about tribal customs until he is about 20, when he is initiated in a ceremony, held every fifth year. Then he becomes a member of the lowest age-set. As he gains more respectability and more social status with the senior age-sets his training and his tasks become less severe. He is free then to marry and no longer has to stay in the men's house. As he grows older he becomes one of the village authorities. Finally he acts as an advisor.

The Paiwan and Rukai of southern Taiwan, who have a more or less similar culture to the other tribes, are the only aboriginal tribes who divide their population into two social classes of nobles and commoners. The chief of a village is the noble with the highest genealogical seniority. Sometimes a chief extends his rule over several villages. He is the landowner. The commoners are obliged to give the chief some part of their produce. It is said that the sun descended to a mountain top and produced two eggs, one red, one white. The eggs were bitten by a spirit snake and a man emerged from one, and a woman from the other. They were the ancestors of chiefly families. Commoners came from the eggs of a green snake. The ruling class has more time for artistic activity. Paiwan and Rukai are skilled in embroidery, appliqué, beadwork, woodcarving and stone sculpture.

The Yami, who live on the small island of Botel Tobago, some 45 nautical miles off the southern tip of Taiwan, have remained isolated from the various influences of Chinese and western civilizations. Cultivable land on their small island is scarce and fishing rules every aspect of their lives. Their plank-built boats are waterproof, sturdy and elaborately decorated. The Yami have been described as a peaceful, friendly and humorous people entirely without warlike spirit. Their weapons and their protective charms and rituals defend them not against human enemies, but against evil spirits – the *anito*. *Anito* are the spirits of the dead and are feared and hated by the whole tribe. When they are away from their own village the Yami carry their weapons with them to do battle with any *anito* they may meet on the road. The Yami's main ceremony is the launching of a new fishing boat. At the end of their ceremony the *anito* must be driven away. Men surround the boat and make threatening gestures, contort their faces, swing their arms and noisily stamp their feet. It is an occasion which possibly offers the Yami their outlet for aggression.

Of all the Malayo-Polynesian peoples the Taiwan aborigines have been least influenced by Buddhism, Christianity, Mohammedanism and Hinduism. Their original cultures, through their contact with the Chinese for hundreds of years and with the Japanese for half a century, have been rapidly dying out. During the 50 years of Japanese rule from 1895 to 1945 government policy was to protect the aborigines from exposure to modern civilization. Tribal territory was reserved. A special permit was required to enter it and the aborigines themselves were forbidden to leave it. Some innovations were enforced. The tribal settlements were shifted to lower land. Wet-rice agriculture and cattle were introduced. Headhunting, tribal warfare, indoor burial and infanticide were banned. Today, although aboriginal land may still be entered only with special permission, the tribal peoples are free to leave it.

Taiwan has a relatively high standard of living; 80 per cent of rural families now own all or part of their land. But the island's greatest hope for accommodating its rapidly growing population is through industrialization. Although the policy is to assimilate aborigines into Taiwan Chinese society their different economic skills prevent them from becoming fully absorbed. Even the so-called sinicized or plains tribes have not fully assimilated Chinese characteristics, though they have lost their own languages, speak Chinese and have Chinese-style ancestor tablets in their homes. Their lives do not revolve around the concept of interest, for example, by which the Chinese so skilfully handle their economic affairs.

Each Paiwan family has its
own house of stone with a
slate roof. It indicates
social status and is
inherited by the eldest son.

Boat people Hong Kong

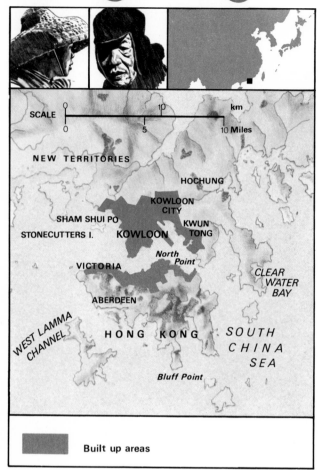

SCALE

NEW TERRITORIES

HOCHUNG

KOWLOON CITY

SHAM SHUI PO

KWUN TONG

STONECUTTERS I.   KOWLOON

VICTORIA

North Point

CLEAR WATER BAY

ABERDEEN

WEST LAMMA CHANNEL   HONG KONG   SOUTH CHINA SEA

Bluff Point

Built up areas

The boat people of Hong Kong are well-known to every traveler to the Far East. Hong Kong's harbor is circled by green hills and by skyscrapers, crisscrossed by ferry services, lined with the berths of ocean-going steamers and staked out with their anchorages. And it is everywhere alive with hundreds of small local craft, most of them powered with diesel engines today, but which only twenty years ago would all have been under sail: lighters, cargo carriers, pilot boats, sampans, fishing boats. Each one of these local boats, or junks – the English version of a Portuguese version of a Chinese word for 'boats' – does double duty as means of livelihood and home for a family of anything from two to thirty-two boat people. At the last census (1971) there were 10,908 people living on boats in Hong Kong, of whom about 5,000 were engaged in one of the world's largest fishing industries.

The Hong Kong boat people differ little from the boat people of all south China. South China fishermen and their families have lived out their lives on boats for as long as there are records to prove it. Generations of fathers, mothers, children and grandparents have lived on board

their fishing boats, living in effect on what are today major instruments of production in one of the world's largest and most highly specialized fishing industries. They own, traditionally, nothing on shore. They have for generations given birth, married and died on board their boats. Only burials are conducted on land. Only the dead live permanently on land. Few boat people have known any other home but their boats. They go barefoot. They are sunburned. They dress almost uniformly in black. They wear distinctive, wide straw hats with turned-down brims. For centuries they have represented a link between south China and the rest of the world.

The Hong Kong boat people represent a major part of the large group of southern Chinese boat people often known to others as Tanka or 'Egg Familes' (which has a derogatory connotation), and to themselves, more accurately, as Shui Min Yan, or Water Surface People. Until recently, it seems, by no means all fishermen, and certainly no fisherwomen, learned to swim. In some places, as for example in the village in the Yangtze Plain described by Fei Hsiao-t'ung, boat people and land people are regarded as being fundamentally alike. In many other places they have been traditionally regarded as a race apart, definitely 'different' from – and inferior to – the land people in almost every respect. Anthropologists who have studied them have no doubt that, whatever their origins the Water Surface People have long been as sinicized, physically, socially, culturally and linguistically, as most of the other Chinese inhabitants of Kwangtung and Kwangsi. With one or two exceptions of a ritual nature (connected mainly with weddings and ancestor worship) their few distinguishing characteristics all stem directly from their water-borne way of life. In Hong Kong today, however, many people sincerely believe that the boat people have always been so radically different – racially, linguistically and culturally – from the rest of the Chinese that they cannot strictly be classed as Chinese at all.

It is commonly said, for example, that because one can usually tell a boat person simply by looking at him, it proves that there is a marked racial distinction between the boat people and the land people. This statement is sometimes followed by another, claiming that boat people always have webbed feet (useful for living on water) or, in another version, that they always have six toes on each foot and six fingers on each hand. The fact that, like many other people in the east, the boat people often go barefoot – giving the lie to these allegations – is overlooked.

Again, one is often told that the boat people speak a non-Chinese language unintelligible to ordinary landsmen. In fact boat people everywhere speak a local (usually Cantonese) dialect. The difficulties in communication which do arise can all be explained in one of three ways: the landsman may be totally unacquainted with the specialized, and rather limited, vocabulary appropriate to boats, fishing and the sea; he may be

50

(Right) From this floating city, home to 10,000, the Hong Kong boat community is rapidly losing many families to new apartments and factories.

Characteristic of Hong Kong enterprise is a floating restaurant on board a junk, for boat people or adventurous tourists.

puzzled by the variety of accents to be found in any given harbor, for the great mobility of the water people will bring fishermen to a harbor whose places of origin and mother-dialect are unknown to the more local land people; and then also some of the boat people, perhaps warned by the centuries of treatment as inferiors, perhaps engaging in illegal activities of one kind or another, have developed forms of secret language which, though simple in theory and all based upon local languages, can, when spoken fast, mystify the uninitiated.

Today, in south China, as in Hong Kong, the generations-old life of the boat people is changing. Not everywhere at once, but steadily and probably irreversibly. In China and in Hong Kong the boat people are going ashore. And as they do so all the customs which have arisen from their water-borne way of life will irrevocably disappear.

Romantic though it often seems to outsiders, and cheerful as the boat people nearly always are, life on board a boat, especially a small one, is actually cheerless and uncomfortable. For women particularly, suffering sometimes from sea-sickness and constantly worrying about toddlers falling overboard, and having to cook, wash clothes, clean and sew in a restricted space, are thankful for the opportunity to move into a building on solid ground. Food is more varied when the street market is round the corner instead of a day's sail away. Lots of fresh water comes from a tap. And it may be possible to add to the family income by doing outwork for a factory. Babies can be born at the clinic. And, above all, the children can go regularly to school.

Boat people's low status derived in the past from their inevitable lack of education. More than once during the imperial era they were officially classed, with actors and other low types, as people who were not permitted even to attempt the imperial examinations. Although this legal restriction was lifted more than 200 years ago for the boat people there was still little chance of sending their children to school for schools were on land. Landsmen despised the boat people and boat people distrusted the landsmen. Most elementary schooling was moreover organized on the basis of clans to which the boat people, although they had exactly the same system of surnames as the landsmen, did not belong. Even had the schools been available to them few boat people would have thought it worthwhile to pay school fees for boys who could be better employed helping with the family business. But since the end of World War II education has quite suddenly become a top priority. Every boat family now wants to send its children to school.

In 1950 virtually all the Hong Kong based fishing craft were driven by the wind. By 1970 more than 85 per cent were mechanized. The boats are now less picturesque, more noisy and more smelly. They are also faster, safer and much more productive. Many a fisherman found that by installing an engine he could double, sometimes even treble, his annual income. And mechanization requires education.

In the crowded anchorages where the family boats have to be used as kitchens and are always occupied, there is a great danger of fire and it is illegal to install a petrol engine. Only inboard diesel engines are allowed. Every mechanized boat therefore automatically comes under the regulation which requires it to carry a licensed engineer and a navigator. To obtain a license it is necessary to study for certain examinations with the result that unless a boat owner is willing to pay high wages to an outsider, at least one member of his family must have four to five years' schooling.

The new methods of selling fish, too, require the use of written receipts. And new co-operatively organized methods of obtaining loans, requiring written records, have been developed by the official Fish Marketing Organization. For the first time education is clearly of the highest practical use to all the boat people. Good, modern schools with qualified teachers have been built in the major fishing villages, provided by the Fish Marketing Organization. In one village in 1950 there was only a single class, only occasionally attended by a few fisher-

Hong Kong's future looms on a bleak horizon — no-one pretends that the colony can survive when the lease on the New Territories expires in 1997.

Boat people are distinguished by their black clothes and wide-brimmed straw hats, not by webbed feet or six toes as the land people say.

(Below) A young family are happy in their floating home, but as the children grow they will almost certainly move ashore — nearer to schools.

men's sons, held intermittently in a tumble-down room beside the local temple. The same village by 1970, with a population hardly changed, had a purpose-built school, with three classrooms, a teachers' residence attached, three trained teachers and a school roll of about 80 boys and girls, all of them fishermen's children.

It is still true, however, that many boat people's children cannot go to school regularly because their floating homes have to move away from time to time in the course of their work. The lucky ones are those whose fathers mechanized their boats early and built small houses ashore with their increased incomes. In some places in Hong Kong blocks of flats have been built for the boat people in which the older members of the family whose working days are over, stay with the mothers, babies and school-age children. In these households only the able-bodied now go to sea. With an engine in the boat fewer hands are needed. Though under a different political and economic system, and with different motives, in China the process is essentially the same. Living in houses and blocks of flats, going to school, and doing shore jobs, the boat people are rapidly becoming assimilated into the Chinese land population. 53

People of Hong Kong

In 1842 Hong Kong was described as 'a barren island with hardly a house on it'. Land today sells for $800 a square foot.

To the hundreds of thousands of tourists who visit Hong Kong each year there is an undeniable beauty in the curving coral beaches of Hong Kong island and the pattern of islands in the South China Sea. And on the New Territories, those islands which lie to the west of Hong Kong and the part of the mainland which rises beyond Kowloon, there are living relics of a 14th century world. In parts it seems that the old China of the emperors is preserved here, in ancient villages, in monasteries and temples, in the valleys between the green paddy fields where women work in great straw hats under a strong sun. But above all, it is the charm of Hong Kong island itself and the great city of Victoria lying on its northern coast opposite Kowloon which draws the visitor. Here in the streets littered with pavement stalls and shops, the tourists discover the orient, bustling and smelling of things Chinese. Yet Hong Kong, despite its 4 million Chinese inhabitants and its physical position as a part of China, is a British colony, an enclave in the east.

The anomalies begin here. Hong Kong is not an ordinary colony. The larger part of its territory is only on loan to Britain – until 1997. The colony lives under sentence of death. No one pretends that the waterless islet of Hong Kong and the crowded knuckle of Kowloon can survive without the adjoining New Territories. But in Hong Kong the people have taken hold of life with a febrile intensity. They have turned their doomed home into a Genoa that out-trades and cut-prices the ends of

54

Mr Run Run Shaw, head of the Shaw Brothers movie empire stands in a street, scene of many a Chinese warrior's bloody end.

the earth, swelling in wealth and magnificence and a unique vulgarity. Hong Kong leads an economic life that is girdled in one of the philosophies of the 19th century – *laissez faire,* the principle of free trade. Hong Kong's industry is dynamic and has produced tremendous growth and huge riches. But like the industrial miracles of 18th and 19th century England the benefits are not seen by all who contribute to industry. And to take the story a little further back, the economic prosperity which first established Hong Kong as a trading center was based upon a single commodity – opium. Although men and companies who made their fortunes in opium traffic have turned to more prosaic and benign trade, the legacy of those early years persists in Hong Kong.

The gay shopping centers are overlooked by the proud rise of tall resettlement apartment blocks built for the refugees who have flooded in from the Chinese republic. Some 800 ships a month discharge or embark their cargoes. But for peasants of Hong Kong the price of living in a free society is grave overcrowding and wages which may be higher than China's but are often low against the enticements of a consumer society. Among the common ills that beset Hong Kong, those like over-

crowding and tenement slums where whole families live in a single room 12 feet square, drug addiction is one that draws the attention of the world. On the hills above Kowloon, where thousands live in tumble-down shacks, the opium is smoked in *divans* which may be no more than an upturned crate on a rooftop or in the mouth of a cave. What these *divans* lack in comfort they make up for in security, for elaborate systems of signals and watchers guard the occupants from the police. And the occasional police raid that does succeed is even likely to be a pre-arranged affair between the drug syndicates and the police concerned for their crime detection rate.

The other addiction is gambling, which some Chinese would say is a basic human tendency, but to the government of Hong Kong is a constant problem. The Chinese even treat the Stock Exchange as another form of gaming and this leads to spectacular rises and falls in share prices, ruin for some and riches for others.

In spite of their addiction the traditional Chinese attitude is that gambling is all right at home, but that publicly accepted legal gambling is too tempting to young people. They habitually gamble at home, playing mahjong with family and friends, and this is tolerated – 55

People of Hong Kong

In spring ancestors' graves are cleaned and evil spirits driven out. Continuity and unity of the family are great strengths in Chinese life.

As many as 500 resettled slum dwellers crowd each floor of government-built blocks. Many regard them as no great improvement on shantytowns.

unless the victim of a *tin-sin-kuk* or 'heavenly swindle' complains to the police. Another accepted form of gambling is the government-run lottery, but the *tse fa* lotteries – illegal but almost traditional – have a hold on the back streets.

Gaming houses are registered as sports associations and the dice and cards quickly hidden when the police arrive. Hundreds of raids on gambling dens are made each year and thousands of convictions follow. Only Macao, the Portuguese province on a peninsula at the mouth of the Canton river, has legal gambling and Chinese from Hong Kong are frequent visitors.

Hong Kong was first occupied by the British in 1841 but was not legally ceded to them in perpetuity until the following year, at the end of the First Opium War with China. The reaction to this annexation in London was on the one hand embarrassment – for the 'barren island with hardly a house on it' did not seem to the Foreign Office a just reward for winning the war with China. But to the British opium merchants who operated in the South China Sea, the annexation of Hong Kong was a boon. With Hong Kong as their base, an island envisaged as a free port, the merchants expected their trade to flourish. And flourish it did. Despite moral

56

As well as exotic eastern wares many tourists find they can buy western products more cheaply than in their own countries, for Hong Kong is a free port.

(Right) War and revolution flooded Hong Kong with refugees who crowd into shantytowns on the hillsides of Victoria and Kowloon.

People of Hong Kong

Kowloon backstreets are like a part of old China. The houses cluster together too closely for anything as modern as a car to pass between them.

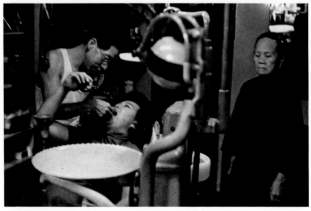

Dentist and patient — are they refugee or communist? many communists hold positions of authority and travel freely to Peking.

A vast selection of false teeth. The plastic they are made from is one of Hong Kong's biggest exports together with textiles and consumer goods.

It is said that any street
urchin will tell you where
to buy opium or, for a few
cents, run and fetch a
small packet of the drug.

objections of the new governor of the colony to drug trafficking, it was justifiably felt that to forbid the importing of opium would be utterly ineffective and only drive the traders elsewhere. The governor issued an edict which neatly sidestepped the issue and only banned smuggling.

The next governor of Hong Kong was forced to give up the struggle against opium traffic. Finding it impossible to restrict, he concluded that it could be better controlled through the legal process and taxation, and turned into a source of revenue for the island. At least one member of the administration objected to 'taxing vice for revenue' but by this time Hong Kong's position as a major opium mart made the temptation of drawing income from it irresistible. In 1844 the governor reported to London that 'almost every person possessed of capital who is not connected with government employment is employed in the opium trade.' By 1906 the trade was worth £5 million ($12·5 million) a year, and contributed some 2 million Hong Kong dollars (by way of opium licenses and licensed *divans*) to the colony's revenue. The use of the drug in Hong Kong itself was not finally made illegal until World War II. By then the wheel had turned full circle: the addiction that opium traders had nourished and

encouraged in China had now fallen upon thousands of residents in the colony. The cost of crime and drug-rehabilitation programs (though these have proved dramatically more successful than others elsewhere in the world) was already high. Only the traders still profited by turning their attention to other commodities, and by beginning to invest the colony with a new, quite different prosperity.

Hong Kong is still essentially a refugee city. Almost half the Chinese population was not born there. Over the years it has been filled with refugees from the mainland, and although the New Territories provide much extra land, most of the people live in the two conurbations of Victoria and Kowloon. At the end of World War II the influx of refugees had ceased and Hong Kong's population fell to some 500,000 as many returned to the mainland. But the Communist Revolution in China in 1949 brought a new stream. The majority were villagers and townspeople from Canton and Kwangtung province, but others – including industrialists, businessmen, academics and professional men from cities like Shanghai – arrived from all over China. Almost all settled in Victoria. The traditional China trade had diminished since China's internal strife and, following the western embargo at the outbreak of the Korean war, ceased altogether. The economic situation in Hong Kong was only saved by a rapid industrial revolution. The resources were all immediately available: capital, cheap labor in excess, business know-how and enthusiasm. Hong Kong was quick to exploit a new market through its dynamic industry which was fully legitimate in the western world. It was the antithesis of what was happening in the new China just a few miles away.

There were other circumstances which favored investment in industry. There were the relatively high adaptability and diligence of the vast labor force, a weak trade-union organization, a lack of legislation fixing minimum wages and limiting working hours and, perhaps most important, extremely low taxation on business profits. The rapidly growing industries attracted still more refugees from China. Just as thousands had once been deluded by the dreams and artificial happiness of the opium pipe, they were now caught in the web of Hong Kong's dream factory. They had certainly escaped the rigors of communist China, but they quickly also discovered the twilight corners of the free west in Hong Kong. Although there are now better laws governing wages and working hours, the massive number of refugees itself creates huge problems.

Perhaps the most obvious and formidable of Hong Kong's problems is housing. In 1961 a census revealed that some 500,000 people lived in squatter huts, shacks and other wooden structures; 140,000 lived in bed spaces; 70,000 in verandas and cocklofts; 56,000 on rooftops; 50,000 in shops, garages and staircases; 26,000 in boats; 20,000 on the streets; 12,000 in basements and 10,000 in 59 stalls and caves. In 1953 a new Resettlement Department had been established by the Hong Kong government, and resolved to exploit the scarce land more fully. They began to build the six-storey concrete blocks which are now so familiar on the skyline.

Resettlement tenants live in standard units of 120 square feet, 24 square feet for each adult and 12 square feet for each child. The walls, ceilings and floors of each unit are concrete. Windows have wooden shutters. The single door leads out onto a balcony which serves as a thorough-fare for the whole floor. Each unit or room houses at least five people, and not always members of the same family. Much family life necessarily spills over onto the balcony and the stairs. Each floor in the block, where as many as 500 people may live, has only one sanitation unit with taps but no basins, and separate latrines for men and women. Some tenants work in their rooms producing articles for small 'cottage' industries.

The resettlement blocks do, however, have their positive aspects like low rents, rooftop primary schools, clubs, playgrounds and clinics. But the drawbacks are obvious and chronic. It is often said that life is healthier in the squatters' huts, in spite of the absence of sanitation and running water, than in the resettlement blocks. In Hong Kong the green hillsides bristle with these white blocks; washing hangs motionless in the stuffy air from the crowded, rusty balconies.

Other factors, however, contribute to the general condition of life. The Chinese do not attach a high priority to living in accommodation which westerners would consider essential for health and comfort. Savings, clothes, jewelry, the outward signs of wealth and status, rank higher than good housing. Once the Chinese in Hong Kong have found a place in which to cook, sleep and keep their possessions, it is enough.

In Hong Kong the Chinese man spends by far the greater amount of the day outside his home. He tends to eat at work, at cooked-food stalls or in restaurants. His hours of work are long. Whether he works in a textiles factory, in the food, paper or printing industry, or making toys or transistor radios, he is likely to be better off than his fellows who work in traditional trades like wood-carving or embroidery. Many men sleep on their employer's premises. Again, here, it is frequently said that the Chinese are very different from westerners in that they place less value on privacy. The Chinese in Hong Kong do not seem to resent living under the curious scrutiny of their neighbors and relatives. Space for children is less a problem than it would be in other communities for children are not encouraged to play games. Even where land is plentiful, as in the villages of the New Territories, houses are not spacious. By contrast there are thousands of Hong Kong Chinese who, by any standards, live in luxury and thousands more who aspire to those same conditions. By and large Hong Kong Chinese have remained essentially Chinese in spite of all the western, colonial and British influences. These influences show themselves most obviously in the use of the English language which dominates commercial life in the colony. There are three times as many children in English language secondary schools as there are in the Chinese schools. The Chinese used is Cantonese which creates a problem for the minorities like the Hoklo speakers from China's eastern Kwangtung province.

Is Hong Kong primarily a western-type city with a host of Chinese trimmings thrown in? The old man with a goatee beard, the beautiful Chinese girls dressed in slit *cheong-sams,* the Chinese slogans above the stalls lining the streets, the temples tucked away in corners of the city, the festivals with parades of Chinese dragons, lantern-bearers and acrobats – all these are clearly Chinese. Miniature skyscrapers, the English language, hectic traffic, the preoccupation with money – the emphasis here is western. In this hard-headed community, in the thronged streets and seething night-life, the answer quickly emerges. The westernization is superficial. A western visitor at a hotel asks the telephone operator for room service. He is answered in Chinese. He asks 'Is this room service?' and is answered with 'Hello'. The visitor repeats 'Is this room service?' and is then answered with silence and heavy breathing – until he hangs up ex-asperated. At first the visitor explains this to himself in terms of the language barrier. He soon discovers his error.

The visitor has met the inscrutable east, and will discover its depth if and when he makes a fuss. His irritation will be met with a blank stare. Should an understanding manager sort out the difficulty, things will immediately afterwards return to normal. The visitor will still receive blank replies on the telephone when he asks for room service. The blank reply – on the telephone 'Hello', speaking in Chinese or just silence – and the blank stare are instinctive Chinese reactions to both rudeness and their inability to understand or provide the service demanded. It is all to do with 'face'.

The subject of face to the Chinese in Hong Kong – whether a fear of losing face or of gaining face – is not one they freely discuss or even contemplate. It is instinctive. Combined with one other factor, the traditional view that the Chinese way of doing things is not simply the best way but the *only* way, face explains a great deal and also reflects the extent to which the Hong Kong Chinese remain Chinese. In almost every conceivable situation the people are concerned about face. A student in a classroom is asked by a teacher to ask questions. The student complies with as few as possible in case he asks a silly one and so loses face. If the teacher insists on more, the student will ask more because to disobey would cause the teacher himself to lose face. It is a factor which makes its contribution to the characteristically Chinese form of patience and reserve, a deep resource, which in Hong Kong – as in China itself – makes for a civic discipline in challenging circumstances unique in this world.

The addict puts his heroin in a foil channel, holds a flame underneath and as the white powder heats, he inhales the fumes through a paper tube.

Lan Tok, aged 50, was sentenced to one year's imprisonment for opium smoking. Wasted by his vice he weighs only 100 pounds.

(Below) By the time he was released Lan Tok had gained 25 pounds. In Hong Kong drug rehabilitation programs have proved dramatically successful.

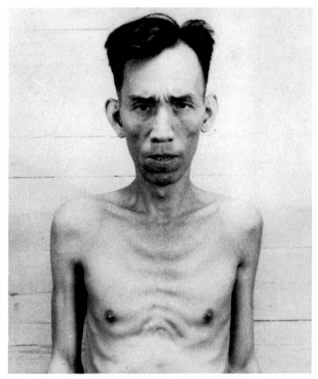

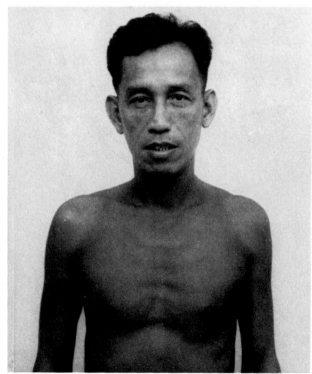

Koreans

Koreans call their country a whale's back which has been damaged in battles between prawns. For centuries the Korean peninsula, between the Sea of Japan and the Yellow Sea, has been invaded from the Manchurian and Chinese mainland. Westward-looking

63

The tall black hat made of
lacquered horse hair is a
Korean status symbol worn
only by the upper classes;
some say even to bed.

Koreans

Although badly damaged in the war of 1950-3, Seoul was rapidly rebuilt to resemble many modern cities with her skyscraping skyline.

64

(Top) Refugees from the North inhabit Seoul shantytowns. Their living conditions are grim; women and children have to queue to buy water.

Korean villagers spend the long winter evenings together. The men make straw shoes, the women sew and all join in the eating and the singing.

Relations between North and
South Korea are improving, but
there is no real trust and
armistice meetings reassemble
again and again.

Japan too has often thought of Korea as the first step into Asia. This history of external threats has given the Koreans a sense of common identity and unity. The Japanese and Manchu invasions in the 16th and 17th centuries were the watershed between Korea's medieval and modern history. To Koreans the centuries seemed to have passed with foreign armies fighting each other up and down the whale's back, their prawn-bitten peninsula.

The Korean peninsula is divided politically at the 38th parallel. Its many mountain ranges cut up the plains. Off the long coast, especially in the south, lie many small uninhabited islands. In this geographically fragmented as well as politically divided country Korean communities have tended to grow in isolation from each other. Although Koreans are conscious, in relation to the rest of the world, of being of one race, each community tends in relation to the other communities to have fostered a feeling of regionalism. For centuries the north Koreans have, for example, been regarded as commoners. And in the 10th century the founder of Korea's Koryo dynasty warned his successors not to trust the people of the south-west. He said their land was convoluted and from it sprang men with twisted hearts.

The 45 million Koreans – 13 million in the north and 32 million in the south – are of Mongolian stock. They feel particularly distinguished as a race from their neighbors by their language and by their dress. Their language is classified as Tungusic (Siberian) by its structure, but cannot be related to any other language by its vocabulary, except for the cultural words which are modeled on Chinese. Although Korean dress may derive from some Chinese style of long ago, the Koreans refused to adopt the styles of the 17th century Manchu invaders.

Both men and women wear short jackets over blouses with baggy trousers which they tie at their ankles. Men wear another fuller jacket on top, and the women a long flowing skirt over their trousers. Many Koreans now wear overcoats, either traditional or western in style, which were once worn by the upper classes. They also wear soft western-style hats. The only traditional hat which serves any practical purpose is the wide straw hat which protects the wearer against rain or sun, today worn by the laboring classes, but once worn only by the upper classes when they were in mourning for a parent and were forbidden to show their faces to heaven. The hat the upper classes usually wear is made of lacquered horse hair. Koreans gleefully tell you that men used to wear these hats not only indoors but also in bed. Korean women, unless they are shamans, seldom wear hats. This is because they carry all their burdens on their heads so that their backs are free to carry children and their hands are free to do house and farm work all at the same time. Men rarely carry anything, but when they do they strap A-shaped wooden frames on their backs.

Koreans are sociable, gregarious and outgoing. They neither respect each other's privacy nor expect their own to be respected. Nevertheless in the towns Koreans seldom entertain much at home. The men leave their wives at home and gather in restaurants or bars where they talk and drink *makkolli* (rice beer) or spirits late into the night. Korea is very much a man's country. Korean men have a favourite saying: 'Male and female over six years do not keep company.' When Koreans do invite people to their homes, however, the guest is welcome to stay as long as he pleases.

It is different in the country. Here families always entertain at home. In the winter evenings the whole village community gathers together in one house. Men and women sit apart, the men making straw shoes and the women sewing. The house is filled with talk and singing – which the Koreans love. At midnight everyone sits down to feast, then everyone goes home.

Korean houses are enclosed by a wall or fence and built with the floors raised about two feet off the ground. Inside there is one room for the master of the house and others for his wife and children. The floor of the room in which the family entertains guests is usually of wood. The others are of packed earth. All the floors have flues running under them heated by the fire. In the winter a guest to a Korean house will be offered the 'lowest' place – on the floor – because that is where it is warmest. The family sleep cosily on the floor covered with thick quilts. Soups and stews simmer 24 hours a day on the fire. This is not only economical but a great comfort when the family wakes up on bitterly cold winter mornings.

All the months from November to March are continually cold in Korea except along the south coast. In January the temperature falls below freezing all over the peninsula. Heavy snow falls in the north and east. July and August, by contrast, are extremely hot and wet. Most of the rain falls in the south. In between these two extreme climates are the dry spring and autumn. For the success of their rice crops Korean farmers depend on a good rainy season at the right time. October and November are the busiest months for the farmer's wife. Before the cold sets in, when nothing edible will grow, 65

Although Koreans love bright
colors they call themselves
'white clothed people'.
White is the color of
sacredness and for mourning.

she washes, soaks and chops mounds of cabbages and
turnips again and again, sprinkles them with red peppers,
and leaves them in brine in a large pot. This highly spiced
preserve is called *kimchi*.

In Korean the word for 'food' is the same as that for
'rice, boiled and ready for eating'. The basis of the
Korean diet is rice with vegetables, with very small
quantities of poultry, pork and game. They eat eggs
mixed up with other foods rather than as separate dishes.
The biggest meal is breakfast on a working day. The
working man's breakfast starts with soup, vegetables
and a little meat all served together, followed by a
separate course of rice. Lunch, which the wives carry out
to their men in the fields, is usually just a snack. Koreans
rarely drink tea or coffee; they drink cold water, or water
boiled up with roasted barley, but at most meals they
simply stir water into the burnt rice at the bottom of the
pan and drink it.

Korean families tend to be large, but close-knit.
When a baby is born his birth is recorded with six
Chinese characters: two each for the hour, day and year
of his birth. His family gets a soothsayer to make up a
name for him professionally. This name either com-
pensates for some threat of disaster at his birth or

66

(Below) Family graves are
important and tended with
great respect. Records of
births and deaths are
also meticulously kept.

strengthens some promise of success. The baby's ancestors, whose tablets are kept by the family in a small room, are informed of his birth. All ancestors are kept up to date with important family news and are addressed several times a year, and always at New Year.

Traditionally Koreans have always regarded education as extremely important. Formerly, unless he had a degree which required a sound knowledge of Chinese classics, a Korean could not become a civil servant. And at one time no other work but that of a civil servant was considered suitable for a gentleman. Farmers, although theoretically respected by Confucianists, were in fact despised and exploited. Any other occupation, from soldier, trader, laborer and scribe, right down to butcher, actor or shaman was considered completely beneath human dignity. This traditional outlook has left its mark and Koreans still value education highly. There are many private teachers who have made small fortunes.

Korean boys and girls usually marry in their late teens. The family consults a marriage broker who seeks a partner of suitable family and time and date of birth. Even in the modern city where young couples are increasingly consulted before being married off, the final decision depends on what the broker discovers from a soothsayer. Except in a few smart families, a wife who does not produce a son will turn to Buddha for help, or, more practically, to the local monk. The allegation that the monk's help is seldom purely spiritual is too often made to be denied with absolute conviction. The childless wife who prays and fasts for 100 days is one of the mainstays of the local Buddhist temple.

The Buddhist 'church', particularly in the 12th to 14th centuries, was rich and powerful. However 15th century neo-Confucians successfully relegated Buddhism to the status of a popular supersision, and it has never since risen from that level. Korea also has Christianity. There are millions of sincere devoted Christians throughout the peninsula. It is difficult to know what the state of either Buddhism or Christianity is in North Korea under the communism which the Russian army imported in 1945. However it seems unlikely that Buddhism which has been Korean for over 1,500 years can have died out within less than one generation.

In South Korea, alongside Buddhist and Christian beliefs, there exists the even older and deeper belief in shamanism. Korean shamans are always women, who wear a headdress which may derive from a Confucian crown. A family calls a shaman into the house after a death or because of illness – always when something has gone wrong – never to celebrate a happy occasion. The thought of summoning the local shaman *(mudang)*, sends a shiver down a Korean's spine. She is a medium who contacts either family's ancestors, who will be a strong ally against the spirits which are causing the misfortune, or she confronts the hostile spirits directly and persuades or orders them to stop their mischief.

Korean religious life is dominated by the teachings of Confucius. Musicians celebrate his birthday by playing tunes on wooden 'tone chimes'.

Hill peoples of Yunnan
China

The dress of Akha women distinguishes them from other hill people — all of whom are quite distinct from lowland Chinese and Tai.

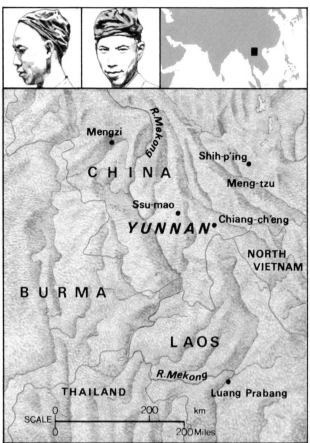

The claim frequently voiced by the People's Republic of China – that the peoples of China are one great family of unity and fraternity – is not accurate in terms of race. Some 94 per cent of the population are Han Chinese. But the remaining 6 per cent who belong to one of the many national minorities, and who ethnically and by their distinctive ways of life may be regarded as non-Chinese, in fact number 45 million. It is a large minority. There are more than fifty minority groups in all, some of whom number more than a million each. And these peoples are distributed over some 60 per cent of China's vast territory.

China's minority peoples live beyond the Great Wall, in the north and north-west, and in the south-west, in the hill country and plateaux of Yunnan, Kweichow, Kwangsi and Kwangtung. Their distribution on the fringes of China has posed serious difficulties of administration even under the cloak of the Republic. In south-west China, and especially in the rugged mountain lands of the Yunnan, these minority peoples represent a way of life that in ancient times was far more extensive, until they were driven into the inhospitable highlands with the expansion of the Han Chinese early in the Christian era. In the Yunnan the life of the Lahu and the Akha in particular recalls these ancient origins.

69

The Lahu are believed to have originated from somewhere in or near Tibet. The Lahu themselves say that they came from the far north to the Yunnan and then spread further south, driven by pressure from the Chinese. About 250,000 of them now live in China, Burma, Thailand and Laos. The great majority live in the Yunnan-Burma border district. They are a proud people whose way of life leaves little place for the timid or physically unfit. They live by strict codes of behavior which, if broken, can lead to summary execution. Until recently they preserved their autonomy in the mountain lands of the Yunnan. Throughout the 18th and 19th centuries they gained some notoriety as rebels against imperial Chinese rule. They fought many battles with the Chinese on the frontier regions. Initially the Chinese adopted a policy of indirect rule. They administered the Lahu settlements with the help of local headmen who were expected to be submissive to imperial authority and to embrace fully Chinese civilization. By the end of the 19th century the Chinese had resorted to direct rule. The viceroy of Yunnan wrote to the Chinese emperor in 1889 reporting that although the Lahu were formerly a restless tribe of savages living on the fringes of Chinese territory, they had been subdued and were gradually coming under the influence of Chinese civilization.

Chinese efforts to subject the Lahu to their rule drove many of them south into Burma and Thailand. But this movement was probably also due to the Lahu's desire for new lands. As early as 1837 a British traveler noted their presence in Kengtung in Burma. They did not pay taxes, he reported, but instead gave mats and cloths, food and service to the Shan chiefs. It was also said that Lahu and Akha warriors were entrusted by the Shan ruler of Kengtung with the defense of his eastern border.

In the Yunnan, as in Burma and Thailand, the Lahu rely on slash-and-burn agriculture. Whenever possible, however, the men spend their time hunting. The Lahu have the reputation as hunters *par excellence*, using crossbow and poisoned arrows to kill bears and deer, squirrels, birds and even panthers. The title of supreme hunter is avidly coveted by all able-bodied men.

Their villages are usually built above 4,000 feet on flat ridges in the hills. They rarely number more than 25 houses, or about 200 people. Perhaps the most important considerations in choosing a village site are the proximity of a good water supply, high land suitable for growing opium poppies and rather lower land for the cultivation of dry hill rice. Because their fields are exhausted within a few years, due to their slash-and-burn method of cultivating them, the Lahu are semi-nomadic. Their villages must constantly be shifted to new lands in virgin forest.

Lahu villages do not look like permanent settlements. The houses are built of bamboo on stout wooden piles with log steps leading up to an open porch and a thatched roof of grass or leaves. Livestock – chickens, ducks,

The Akha lead a peaceful, organized life. Even in death the soul is turned away from a path of war since 'that path leads to hell'.

(Bottom) Akha children play on a 'spirit swing' which is like the giant swing built each year for the goddess of fertility.

The unmistakable Akha head-dress is created with silver coins, beads, buttons, feathers, and fur – and all is entwined with the girl's hair.

horses, buffalo, cows, dogs and pigs – roam freely beneath the houses. Pigs are by far the most important animals to them as pork is an essential ingredient of their ritual feasts. The households, of parents, children and sometimes grandchildren, are only loosely bound together in the village. Ties of kinship, marriage or friendship may be easily severed when a family moves away.

The village elders elect a headman or 'master of the village' to dispense justice and settle disputes. In a region where there are several villages one headman is often regarded as the senior. He becomes influential and is recognized by more distant authorities – the Shan princess or Chinese mandarins in the past, the district officials today.

The Lahu believe in a great number of spirits, good and bad. The good spirits include the village and house spirits who are protective by nature, but inclined also to be capricious. The bad spirits include the whirlwind and lightning spirits who are thought to be sources of illness and misfortune. Above all these spirits the Lahu believe in a supreme being. The *pawku*, the village priest and the most important of the three Lahu religious specialists, leads the people in sacrifices and ceremonies in honor of this 'father god'. There is also the *mawpa*, or shaman, who is thought to possess occult powers which enable him to discern spirits which cause illness and to exorcise evil spirits and demons. He is able to practise both black and white magic. And there is the medicine man or *shepa* who, by certain rituals and his supernatural healing abilities, is able to discern offending spirits and cure people who have fallen sick because of sorcery.

The legendary history of the Akha, another minority people who live in the Yunnan and in Kengtung (Burma), Laos and Thailand, speaks of seven brothers from whom all the Akha are descended and of seven divisions of their people, all differing somewhat in dress and dialect. Today probably some 50,000 Akha live in the Yunnan. At least as many live across the border with Burma, Laos and Thailand.

The Akha build their villages on steep hills in the Yunnan, usually just beneath the crest of a ridge with their fields, which they also cultivate by slash-and-burn, spread above and below. On the lower slopes tall savanna grass grows through which the Akha cut broad paths. The paths lead to the village gates, which figure prominently in the Akha religious beliefs and sacrifices. On top of the gates stand carved wooden figures and, at the sides, male and female fertility figures. The gates are sacred as the water spirit lives close by them. Bamboo designs on top represent flowers which entice the spirit to stay, while the wooden figures represent birds which supposedly give out a warning whenever evil spirits try to enter the village.

Akha villages are not otherwise fortified or fenced and they are not laid out in any regular fashion. There may be as many as 200 houses in the village – although this would be unusually large for each household includes at 71

Hill peoples of Yunnan China

The Lahu are a proud people.
Until recently they preserved
their freedom in Yunnan
and even now shun contact
with lowland people.

least ten people. The houses, built of bamboo with thatched roofs, are built on the hill slopes with the front portion raised on piles. Inside there may be partitions which divide the sleeping quarters from the working quarters. Every five or ten years the villages are shifted to a new slope – to new areas to slash-and-burn and cultivate – which is rarely more than a day's march away. Sometimes however, the village will move because of an epidemic of sickness which is attributed to the displeasure of local spirits.

The Akha are easily distinguished from the other hill people of the Yunnan because of the appearance of their womenfolk. Akha women wear tall, elaborate head-dresses covered in numerous objects like silver coins, beads, buttons, fur, feathers and even small gourds. The headdresses fall down on either side of the head and are entwined with their hair, which the women only rarely comb. It is even said that Akha women sleep with their headdresses on. The men in contrast cut their hair short, except for a tail at the back. Akha men believe that if this tail were cut bad spirits would be able to enter their heads and make them mad. All the Akha, men and women, young and old, smoke pipes of tobacco. Even out in the fields the women clutch the long bamboo pipe between their teeth and encourage their five or six year old children to smoke.

In their fields, both those which are close to the village and others which may be several hours away, the Akha mix rice with maize, buckwheat, sugar cane, beans and melons and many other crops. Only the ubiquitous opium poppies and tobacco are planted separately. Sometimes marigolds are planted in with the rice so that the women can use these bright flowers in their headdresses. The Akha also hunt with crossbows, like the Lahu, and fish in the rivers with lines, hooks and weirs. They keep numerous domestic animals like pigs and chickens and dogs. Pigs and chickens have special importance as sacrificial food. The dogs, which scavenge the village for all the leftovers, are thought a great delicacy. Some Akha

keep cattle, buffalo and horses, although mainly for trade with people of the lowlands. The Akha are not, however, keen traders with the lowlanders. They shun contact with them and sell their opium instead mainly to the itinerant traders who travel from village to village.

The Akha animistic religion is much like that of the Lahu. But the Akha lay greater stress on ancestor spirits. Some of the spirits are malevolent and cause sickness. Others are associated with familiar objects like trees. There are guardian spirits of the houses and the village. The family ancestor spirits are often represented by a basket kept in the house or by a sacred post. The Akha take great care during the growing season not to offend the rice spirit. The religious practitioners are chosen from those villagers who have shown supernatural powers. Sometimes the office of village chief and priest coincides, but the greater shaman or *tumo* has a hereditary position and is greatly feared and highly respected for his contact with good and evil spirits. He may often extend his power and influence over many villages in a district. Loss of soul is a rare cause of illness, the Akha believe; they more frequently attribute illness to offended or evil spirits. A religious practitioner is thereupon called to divine the nature of the spirit, and then to use his supernatural powers to exorcise it. The Akha have little knowledge of the use of drugs or herbs. Their only practical remedies involve opium and bloodletting – which they probably learned from the Chinese.

There is great freedom of sexual behavior among the adolescent boys and girls in Akha villages. In some villages there is a special courting ground at the edge of the village where the young people gather in the evenings. Here they sing and dance and flirt with one another and there is a constant flashing of torches. Girls run away from the eager boys, often only to lead them to the bushes. Another tradition by which young people are educated in adult ways is both secret and almost obsolete. By this practice adolescent girls are required to submit to a middle-aged widower, selected by the village elders, before they attain marriageable status. This man, known as the *aw shaw*, instructs the girls in the art of love-making. And for the adolescent boys, there is a similar education by a widow, called the *mida*, also chosen by the elders.

For both the Akha and the Lahu the influences of lowland people are increasingly difficult to resist. These people have traditionally responded to poor harvests simply by moving their villages to new sites. Seldom have they remained in one place long enough either to ruin or improve their land. But this kind of shifting agriculture cannot survive population growth and the demands of the Chinese who now govern the Yunnan. Unable to move so freely, the hill tribes are in danger of irredeemably overworking their land. Only by the efforts of the Chinese authorities can one hope that their distinctive cultures will be preserved.

Once the village headman led
his people to war. Now there
is only hunting — for which
Lahu are renowned — and
music, for which they are not.

Tibetans

Much of Tibet's culture
emanates from its monasteries.
The monks help villagers
celebrate festivals and play
their traditional instruments.

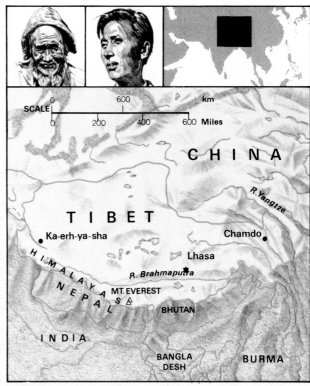

The people of Tibet live on the highest extensive tract of land in the world, on a plateau more than 10,000 feet above sea level. It is arid and cold in winter and, even in the valleys where most Tibetans live, sparsely populated. Farmers and small wandering bands of nomadic Tibetans use the vast stretches of steppe and mountain that lie between the valleys to graze their livestock. There are Tibetans who are neither totally settled nor totally nomadic but stay put in the winter and roam in the summer. All Tibetans, even those who normally lead sedentary lives, love to travel. They go on pilgrimages to holy places and undertake long journeys in pursuit of trade in spite of the bad roads, which are frequently infested with robbers. The monks of the numerous monasteries can often be seen traveling seeking knowledge from scattered libraries and teachers. Also roaming the plateau are the itinerant professionals – the storytellers, the musicians, the physicians and astrologers.

The origins of the Tibetans, who are a racially diverse people, is a mystery. According to their own legends their first ancestors were a monkey and a rock demoness. The children of this union were half-man, half-ape, and had flat red faces and, some say, tails. What is certain is that the Tibetans are related to the Ch'iang. The Ch'iang were western neighbors of the Chinese long before the birth of Christ and still survive on the Sino-Tibetan borders. Tibetans share with Ch'iang the same ideas of 75

Tibetans

Since only the eldest son in a Tibetan family inherits, many, like this boy, join monasteries as young as four or five years old.

(Below) Novice monks are taught to read and write. Those who stay will progress to learn and practise the arts of philosophy and meditation.

Tibetan religious music is usually played by monks. The instruments they play are trumpets, shawms (Tibetan oboes), lutes, flutes and drums.

heaven, ancestry and architecture – monumental stone structures like towers and fortresses. Most Tibetans can easily be taken for Mongols, though individuals have reminded visitors of Japanese, Europeans, Iranians and North American Indians. And there are even a few red- and blond-haired Tibetans. The language they speak, however, is not Mongol at all, but is related to Burmese, to a number of tongues spoken by various Himalayan peoples and ultimately to Chinese. It is split into many dialects and Tibetans often find it difficult to understand each other.

The way of life of a Tibetan farmer and his family is a simple one. Tibetan farming families live in the sheltered valleys in small villages, which are controlled by a headman who organizes the village, collects the taxes and keeps the village accounts. Their houses are square and solidly built of stone, sun-dried brick or pounded earth with a flat roof on which they store fuel and fodder for the winter. In the south and south-west, where more rain falls, their homes have pitched roofs. The family live on the first floor, which is simply furnished. They keep the ground floor for their precious livestock: the cattle, which provide dairy products – an essential part

76

(Right) Prolonged exposure to Himalayan winds makes skin wrinkle. Tibetan women used to protect their faces with *cutch*, a greasy red or black cosmetic.

Tibetans

Before his exile following the Chinese invasion the Dalai Lama lived in the Potala in Lhasa, a palace beautifully decorated with gold engravings.

The Forbidden City of Lhasa would once be approached only by caravans that took months to get there. Today a modern highway makes it an easy trip.

of Tibetan diet – and sheep, goats, pigs and poultry. These animals along with the yak, which is prized highly by all Tibetans, are grazed on the high grounds by the young sons of the family who go off with the animals for days at a time with only a sling and a dog to protect themselves and their herds from the wolves and leopards. While the sons are away the farmer, his wife and daughters tend their small fields, in which they grow a limited variety of crops, mainly wheat, barley, buckwheat, peas, radishes and potatoes. As the summers are brief only a single crop can be harvested. The farmer uses his horses, yaks, mules and donkeys with sheep and goats to carry loads up to the house where the produce is stored for the winter. Until the 1950s the Tibetans used no wheeled vehicles at all. Their simple plow is pulled by yaks or by the *dzo,* a crossbreed of the yak with the common cow, or occasionally even by human beings.

In the village amusements are few. There are visits to the local temple and spontaneous singing and dancing at local festivals and ceremonies. At home people play the flute and guitar or hold competitions in verse-speaking. These verses are usually of four lines and often comment on topical affairs. They are pointed and witty but seldom crude, for the Tibetans love the use of skilful allusion and concealed implications. When, formerly, there were rivalries between neighboring villages the people would hold contests at repartee in verses. The villagers would meet at their common boundary, advance in line and sing their verses, to which the other side had to find an apt reply. Today for other, not self-made, entertainment, the Tibetan villagers rely on the visits of traveling singers and dancers. But these visits are rare and for most of the year the Tibetan farmer and his family are preoccupied with tending their herds and small fields.

The Tibetan nomads who wander the peninsula – unlike the farmers who depend on both their animals and crops – have only their animals to sustain them. They range on horseback with their guard dogs and herds over clearly defined territories which are communally owned. When they stop they set up their camp of black tents. For a few days their settlement becomes a village. The

Tibetan houses are square and solidly built of stone, brick or pounded earth. Roofs are flat or pitched, depending on the amount of local rainfall.

Chinese army trucks make their
way up mountains
16,500 feet above sea level
to bring supplies to their
troops stationed there.

(Below) After the fall of
Lhasa in 1959 the Chinese
staged public trials to
discredit the toppled régime.
This woman is a witness.

women cook, the children play, the dogs rush round and the men repair their saddle gear, count their animals and discuss where next they can find the best grazing. Of all Tibetans the nomads prize and depend on the yak. It is an animal ideally suited to their nomadic life and harsh environment. It is impervious to cold, extremely sure-footed when carrying loads and a useful source of milk. The nomads use its hair to weave cloth for their clothes and tents. And it is a valuable parent for cross-breeding with common cattle. Besides the yak the nomads herd sheep and produce a large surplus of wool, cheese and butter which they trade for grain with the farmers. Most of the nomad groups are gentle and peace-loving, but there are some like the dreaded Golok of the north-east who frequently turn bandit and raid traders' caravans.

Both nomads and farmers are expert at the domestic arts of spinning, weaving and dyeing and make all their own household goods and clothing. Although clothes vary slightly from region to region all Tibetans in the country wear the same kind of garment – a long loose-sleeved coat tied tightly at the waist and worn long by women and shorter by men. The nomads make their coats of sheepskin and wear the woolly side next to their skin to keep the cold out, while the farmers sew it from locally woven homespun cloth. Even the Tibetan aristocrats wear the same kind of coat though they like theirs made in Chinese silks and brocades. For official ceremonies the aristocracy also have a range of brightly colored clothes and hats, some Chinese inspired, others supposedly dating from the time of the early Tibetan kings. Beneath the coat the Tibetan wears trousers, on his feet long felt boots, and on his head a hat with fur-lined flaps. Tibetan women who are married also wear a striped apron and all, whether married or not, love to have spectacular jewelry of gold, silver, coral, amber and turquoise. Formerly women smeared their faces with a black or red cosmetic – *cutch* – a greasy substance imported from India which prevented their skins from becoming desiccated by the wind.

Women have traditionally always held a high position in Tibetan society. They are free both economically and sexually. And, particularly among the settled farmers who make up the majority of the population, they have the most say in family matters and manage the family finances. Among Tibetan farmers the single family households form the basis of society. Most Tibetans view with horror any marriage between possible blood relatives, however distant. Anyone who has the same clan name is assumed to be descended from the same ancestor, and marriage is therefore out of the question. In Tibet a woman is usually married to two or more brothers. She is married formally to the eldest. Then the younger brothers automatically become her husbands as well. Of all her children, whom she may have by all her husbands, the eldest brother is regarded as the father. Her eldest child inherits the family house and

79

Tibetans' hard lives are often enlivened with festivities. Men compete in archery and horse races, women perform dances like this traditional hat dance.

land – or rather the use of them since they are government-owned. The younger sons either marry away, stay and help on the farm or enter a monastery. If a family has no sons a daughter can inherit. Or they may choose to adopt a son. The family invites a man to marry their daughter, change his name to theirs and thus become their heir. This system of inheritance can and does sometimes result in bitter family disputes but on the whole it works. It does tend, however, to produce a surplus of unmarried women, some of whom enter nunneries. It is quite acceptable for Tibetan women to marry two or more husbands who are not related. They may even marry a father and son. And there is little or no stigma attached to pre- or extra-marital sexual relations.

More than anything else it is religion – among the nomads, villagers and townspeople – that dominates a Tibetan's life. Before the arrival of Buddhism the Tibetans had their own religion. Little is known about it but it certainly included the appeasement of a large number of supernatural beings, many of whom were associated with the earth. There was also an elaborate cult centered on the Tibetan kings of the time. Both animals and people were sacrificed to them. Some elements of this old religion were absorbed in Buddhism which saturated Tibetan life from the 13th century.

Mahayana Buddhism – in Tibetan form sometimes called lamaism – arrived from northern India and Nepal. Tibetan Buddhists believe that the lot of human

Tibetans use prayer-wheels to invoke the help of a vast pantheon of gods in attaining their ultimate goal: the stilling of human desires.

(Center) On 1 October Tibetans take to the streets to celebrate the day of declaration of the People's Republic of China.

Women enjoy a high position in Tibetan society. They are economically and sexually free, and often have more than one husband.

beings is a long, miserable round of continual rebirths. Nothing is permanent and suffering abounds. The goal which they strive constantly to reach is the stilling of human desires which leads to the extinction of the human personality in a transcendental state of enlightenment. To achieve this they practise a combination of meditation and ritual and yogic practices. Also they invoke the help of a vast pantheon of supernatural beings which they believe exist in a relative though not absolute sense.

In many areas it is considered customary for boys to enter a monastery at an early age – sometimes as young as four or five. There, as novices, they are taught to read and write and to perform rituals, at the core of which is the chanting of sacred texts. Many leave and return home once they have reached this stage, but others progress to learn and practise the art of meditation, advanced rituals and to study philosophy. The best monasteries are true universities like those of medieval Europe. And it is in these monasteries that class distinctions are at their lowest. Here it is quite common for men from the lowest social class to reach high office.

Allegedly the oldest and greatest of the Tibetan Buddhist orders is the Nyingmapas. In this order there are several distinct kinds of practitioners. There are the celibate monks who live in the monasteries following a strict discipline derived from the traditional Indian Buddhist rules. All are aiming at an ascetic way of life. And the higher a grade a monk reaches so the rules become stricter. Those who reach a sufficiently high level become teachers and are called 'lamas' – the superior ones. Belonging to the same order are local priests, who are allowed to marry, and who perform rituals and ceremonies for the villagers. These rituals are often of a magical nature. The priests drive away hail, illness and any other disaster and also guide the souls of dead men into their new bodies. And finally also belonging to the Nyingmapas order are laymen – farmers in the remote areas of the Himalayas – who when the need arises take up their priestly duties and perform ceremonies in the local temple.

Some Tibetans intent on seeking enlightenment choose to pursue it outside the monastic orders. They become hermits seeking the solitude of caves. These solitaries, often revered by the ordinary people, have been some of Tibet's most famous writers and poets.

The monasteries played an important role in Tibetan culture. Fine and applied arts, particularly painting, metalwork, literature and scholarship, all flowed from the monasteries. The monks did not keep these arts to themselves or within the walls of their monasteries. In the village when rituals were carried out, accompanied by local festivities and entertainments, the monks – clad in masks and costumes – performed fantastic dances to the music of trumpets, shawms (oboes) and drums.

Much of the power and knowledge of the Tibetan monasteries have disappeared in the last 13 years. In the 1950s the Chinese built a number of roads and introduced modern transport to Tibet. In 1959 Tibet was absorbed more fully into China. And in the same year the Dalai Lama, both the religious and secular head of the country, fled into exile. The Chinese rigorously applied communist socialist and economic policies. They closed many monasteries and attempted to collectivize the land. They attempt to confine people to their villages by forbidding them to leave without a special pass. The nomads and the remote villagers have probably been least affected by these changes and for them life continues much as before.

In Tibet the life of most people is hard, but it is still enlivened with many festivities, especially round New Year. The people in the country love to go on picnics. They leave the villages in groups, seek out a place and pitch their tents. Here they prepare large quantities of food and drink. Men and women sing, dance and gamble. The men compete in archery contests and horse races. The music is provided by the *dramnyen,* or Tibetan lute, by flutes and one-stringed fiddles. Such revels may last for days.

Bhutanese

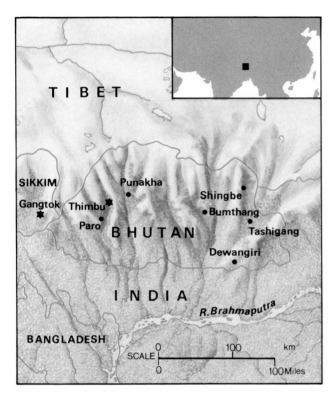

Bhutan is a tiny Himalayan kingdom wedged in between Sikkim, Tibet and India. It has under a million inhabitants. Because of communist China's invasion and subjugation of Tibet the Bhutanese are now among the few people in the world who still practise Tibetan culture. For centuries Bhutan has been isolated. But it has always been strategically important. It is a buffer state between India and China and today India gives Bhutan a subsidy – following the British precedent – in return for advising her on defense and foreign policy. To enter Bhutan one must have the permission of the King and the Indian government.

In the cold north of the country great snow-clad peaks skirt the Tibetan plateau. Among the lesser mountains of middle Bhutan are the valleys where willows and rhododendrons grow. Tibetan invaders were attracted to this land and they established a new system of government there as early as the 8th and 9th centuries. These hills and valleys are not unlike the highlands of Scotland or the foothills of the European Alps. The weather is mild with heavy rainfall and a little snow in winter. It was in these hills that the European first discovered the blue poppy and the rhododendron. In the south of Bhutan are the jungly foothills, where the climate is subtropical: few Bhutanese live here. Most of the inhabitants are immigrant Nepalese families who are settled farmers. They have taken Bhutanese citizenship, but have kept their Hindu religion and their own customs and dress. Away from the southern boundary of Bhutan

82

Bhutanese are among the last upholders of Tibetan culture and are especially famous for their cloth. This may cloak an interior temple wall.

stretches the great plain of the Ganges.

Most true Bhutanese live in the central mountains and valleys. They have absorbed many of the ancient peoples who once lived there and who have left traces of their customs and dialects in certain places. In the east a few tribes, called by the Bhutanese Monpa or Dakpa have remained little affected by Bhutanese culture. There are some Lepcha too, a people who now live mainly in Sikkim. Other small groups include semi-nomadic high-landers in the north who seem even more akin to the Tsang Tibetans over the border than are the Bhutanese. There are descendants of former slaves captured in India who are distinguished by their music, and there are recently arrived Tibetan refugees who have been settled in communities on the land or who live by trade.

Almost all Bhutanese have black hair and dark brown skins. The men grow little hair on their faces except for thin drooping moustaches which grow from the outer edges of the upper lip. Some have little goatee beards. They spend hours with tweezers and mirrors plucking out offending hairs that grow in the wrong places. They have solid, well-defined bone-structures, with narrow eyes and thin lips. Nearly all Bhutanese women have their heavily fringed black hair cut short like their men. They do as much, if not more, manual work as the man and this, combined with years spent in pregnancy, means that many of them look prematurely old. It is hard to assign the Bhutanese to one physical type for mongoloid, Indoaryan and South-east Asian strains are clearly discernible. Most of the Bhutanese speak Tibetan dialects although there are many non-Tibetan words, especially in the east.

Rice is Bhutan's staple crop but it does not grow above 7,000 feet. Above this altitude the staple is buckwheat, which is ground into flour and made into round cakes. Rice is grown in small irrigated fields in the valley bottoms. In winter the fields are left fallow. Higher up the slopes cattle graze in the scrub and forest. Around the houses black pigs and a few chickens wander about. The chickens lay only a few small eggs since, like the pigs, they feed off nothing but the household scraps. The main vegetable is red pepper, liberally used to spice the rice dishes. Up in the high altitudes the Bhutanese keep yak – used mainly for transport – and goats, but not many sheep. All over Bhutan wild foods from the forests are collected to supplement the diet. It is a diet which is good by Asian standards and consists mainly of pork, eggs and vegetables. Tea and Tibetan beer are the main drinks.

Among the local dishes are *chura, tsampa* and *churpi*. *Chura* is made by heating fried rice in tea until it has swollen. *Tsampa* – a food common in Tibet – is made from finely ground barley. The barley flour is put into butter tea and stirred slowly with the finger until it has formed a soft porridge. *Churpi,* the ideal hard ration, is cheese beaten and dried until it is of rock-like consis-

tency. Then it is strung in small lumps like a necklace. You cannot bite into it but have to keep it in the mouth and suck until, after a long time, the outside softens enough to produce a tiny layer of cheese. One piece, not much bigger than a sugar lump, might take an hour to eat.

In peasant households meals are eaten on the floor with the food dished out of a great pot. The people in the north do not fare as well as those in the rest of Bhutan. Their wheat crops are meager and their cattle are leaner than elsewhere. But nowhere do cows produce much milk since there is no cultivated grass for them and fodder is poor. They are thin, hardy beasts with small udders. The little milk that is produced is rarely drunk as such, for the people turn it into butter. Not even young children are given milk to drink. As Buddhists the Bhutanese do not slaughter cows for meat, but only eat them if they die of old age or naturally, perhaps falling over a cliff. The flesh is cut into strips and left in the sun to dry until it is as hard as leather thongs. It will then keep indefinitely. Betel nut is chewed throughout Bhutan and most people's teeth are stained dark red.

There are few tractors or other modern farming implements in Bhutan. Most people till their fields either by hand, using a mattock and then a rake, or else they plow them with two oxen harnessed to a broad yoke. The fields are small and cut up by irrigation channels fed by the numerous small rivers and streams that flow down the mountainsides. The main fertilizers are burnt wood chippings and dead leaves. Dried cow dung as well as wood is used for fuel.

Bhutanese dwellings are large for they are built to house not only family but animals and stores as well, rather like Swiss chalets. They are at least two storeys high and often four or more. The walls of the lower floors are up to four feet thick and are made of earth rammed between boards on a stone foundation. Girls may often be seen on the walls with long wooden rammers beating down the mud and singing as they work. The upper storeys are of a wooden framework filled in with wooden panels and wattle-and-daub, and painted white. On top of the flat roof is a second widely pitched roof supported on a heavy wooden frame, leaving underneath an open-sided loft.

Cattle and pigs live on the ground floor of the house. There is often a fence attached to enclose a yard in front. An outside ladder – often just a log with notches cut into it – leads up to the first floor, used for storing grain and other food. Above this are the family quarters. In one large living room is the hearth or stove where the family cooks and eats. As there is no chimney it is often filled with smoke and many of the women especially suffer from inflamed eyes and eyelids. Small bedrooms lead off this room – and a chapel which is often used as a guest room. In the loft above fuel and fodder are stored.

Bhutanese men wear long loose coats like the Tibetans, but rather shorter. The coat is tightly bound round the

There are local administrative and religious centers, called *dzongs*, throughout Bhutan to which horse or mule is the main means of transport.

Buddhist monks of the *Drukpa Kargyupa* order, one of the 'red hat' sects of Tibetan Buddhism, sit in meditation in the serenity of a temple.

Dancing, singing and archery are favorite Bhutanese entertainments. Here a group of antler-topped girls perform the stag dance.

waist above which a loose fold is used as a pocket. In this pocket they usually keep a square of cloth used as a plate for food, a tin of betel nuts and often a heavy straight knife. The wealthier members of society wear long leather boots or nowadays western shoes and socks. But many people go barefoot. A pair of cotton trousers worn under the coat is tucked into the boots or socks. Women's dresses are pinned at the shoulders with large silver brooches joined by a chain. Bhutanese women are excellent weavers and produce a wide variety of cloth patterns from wool, cotton and rough silk on their simple backstrap looms. They make their clothes from striped, checked and embroidered materials, often in bright colors and of complex design, many of which are copied in Indian textile mills.

Until the 1960s there were no towns, as such, in Bhutan. In place of towns were fortified dzongs set amidst the scattered houses in the valleys. Dzongs are civic and religious centers for each region. The largest dzong in Bhutan is the one at Thimbu the capital. It was rebuilt during the 1960s. Like all dzongs it has a central temple block, for a dzong is a place of worship as well as an administrative center. Around the outside of the temple block is usually a large wall and around this a courtyard further enclosed by the outside walls which present a defensive exterior. Many country people send their sons to dzongs for it earns them spiritual merit and a chance of a better reincarnation. At the four corners of the Thimbu dzong are four palaces for the king, the commander-in-chief of the army, the head lama and the monks. In the outside walls are the government offices.

The Bhutanese are wonderful builders and architects. Every stone block of the Thimbu dzong was hand-chiseled. Every timber has been cut and trimmed to an exactness admirable by western standards, with axes and adzes. When building their houses they rarely use a hammer and nails. Occasionally a wooden peg is used but usually beams have simple tenon and mortis joints.

Those who hold high office in the dzong are distinguished by a magenta scarf and a three-foot sword with 85

Bhutanese

On looms like these, outside simple dwellings, beautiful cloths are made. Many patterns are copied in Indian textile mills.

an embossed handle which is presented by the king. Men below a certain rank must bare their legs and all wear sashes colored according to their rank. Traditionally Bhutanese society was stratified into ranks with a hereditary aristocracy carrying out the work of government. As in Tibet there was a strong system of central control. The central government was in the hands of the *Shapdrungs* until 1907 when it was transferred to a line of lay kings, the Dragon Kings. The great grandson of the first of the lay kings came to power in 1952 and died in 1972. While it was being decided which son should rule in his stead, his wife became regent. Nowadays government is more widely based. The king rules with an elected council, which has certain constitutional powers rather then just advisory ones as before. Yet the feudal structures prevail.

By Indian standards Bhutanese society is remarkably free. There is no caste system although a few groups such as blacksmiths and the descendants of former slaves have a particularly low status. There are opportunities for young people to rise to positions of authority in the kingdom. Women in many spheres are the equals of men, and may hold important positions.

In Bhutan there are few marriage laws. A man may have as many wives as he likes, although only a few can afford to keep even two. Alternatively a woman may have more than one husband. This is rare too, except among the upper classes. The commonest form of polyandry is when a woman marries several brothers. There is no need for a formal marriage service in Bhutan. Girls are eligible for marriage from the age of 16 onwards. A couple usually just join up and their union is sealed by the birth of children. They may register their children in the dzong but this is not compulsory. Divorce is simply a matter of parting although it is expensive since the party who leaves must pay heavy compensation. Few can afford to get divorced. All over the country are phallic symbols adorning the balustrades of bridges or the corners of the houses.

After delivering a child a Bhutanese mother puts the placenta in the river or burns it. Then she baths and puts on new clothes. In the following days she has three baths a day for as long as her status demands. The queen for instance baths for 25 days after delivery. After a week or so babies are fed on butter and sugar as well as their mother's milk and they are weaned by being given a little premasticated food.

Archery is the national sport of Bhutan. Wherever a

86

group of men are gathered together an archery contest will sooner or later begin. There are usually six to a team. They all shoot off at a target about one foot wide and three feet high, then they go down and collect their arrows and shoot back to the other end. An exceptionally good shot is greeted by a dance of triumph with the men circling slowly and moving their feet and hands in dance movements. The bows, of about six feet long, are made of split bamboo and the strings of twisted nettle stalks. These are kept wet to maintain maximum tension. The arrows are made of bamboo and tipped with metal. Archers use leather finger guards when shooting.

The Bhutanese are also fond of gambling, music and dancing. And besides their magnificent building and weaving they are good basketworkers, metal workers and woodcarvers. The beautifully carved and painted dragons' heads around the roof of the temple of the Thimbu dzong bear witness to their craftsmanship.

Besides a rich and varied folk culture there is the higher culture provided by Buddhism. The most important order of Tibetan Buddhism in recent centuries has been the *Drukpa Kargyupa* order, one of the so-called 'red hat' sects which has given the country its Tibetan and Bhutanese name – Druk. There are large numbers of celibate monks and dozens of monasteries, some only fully occupied in summer. The monks often enter the monasteries as young children and there they are taught to read and write and perform religious ceremonies. Church and state were integrated in the person of the ruling *Shapdrung* and the monastic establishments still attract respect and prestige. The monastic dances or *cham* are particularly popular in Bhutan. These dances are devoted to the worship of the protective divinities of Tibetan Buddhism. The monks dress in elaborate costumes and masks, and dance to horn music, shawns, drums and cymbals. As well as forwarding their own religious careers in the monasteries the monks may also perform rituals and ceremonies for the layfolk, such as healing ceremonies. Buddhist morality provides the main code of conduct, aiming in the first place at securing a favorable reincarnation in the next life.

In the last two decades Bhutan has developed more contacts with India. Indian goods are on sale in Bhutanese bazaars and inevitably bring changes into everyday life. In the schools knowledge of English is being spread. In the valleys of central Bhutan where formerly only rice was grown there are now orchards of apples, cherries, plums and pears.

But the government is enlightened enough to conserve and adapt as much of the traditional culture as possible without abandoning it in favor of indiscriminate westernization. Most new buildings are adaptations of traditional styles. The pace of change is slow and the Bhutanese have a better chance than most Asian peoples of retaining a genuine cultural distinctiveness based on their ancient and traditional civilization.

Nepalese

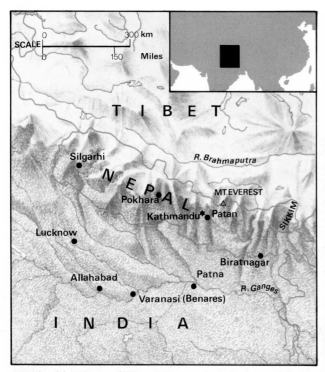

The kingdom of Nepal has a share in two different worlds. The peoples on its northern borders are of mongoloid stock, speak Tibeto-Burman languages and profess the type of Buddhism traditionally associated with Tibet. Racially, linguistically and ethnographically they belong to the part of humanity with which this volume is concerned. Yet, all along the Himalayas and in the maze of rugged hills extending southwards of the snow-covered main range, such people of Tibetan type dovetail and overlap with populations speaking Indo-European languages and representing in their physical make-up the easternmost branch of the europoid race. In most regions these racial and linguistic distinctions coincide with the boundary between the two great world religions Hinduism and Buddhism, and the interaction of disparate ethnic and cultural groups has played an essential part in the formation of a civilization of great complexity.

The people of the kingdom are divided into many castes and tribes, which are socially self-contained units, yet economically dependent on each other. At the apex of the hierarchy stand the high Hindu castes of Brahman, Thakuri and Chetri. They speak Nepali, an Indo-Aryan tongue, and in their physical features bear unmistakable signs of close affinity with the dominant races of northern India. Among their ancestors are the Kha, martial hillmen encountered as early as the 5th century AD in Kumaon, Garhwal and the adjoining regions of Nepal, as well as Rajput warriors who penetrated the Himalayan valleys in several waves when Muslim invaders dislodged them from their Indian homelands. The principalities

88

The Himalayan Kingdom of
Nepal bridges two worlds: here
mongoloid and Indo-European
peoples, Buddhists and Hindus
all meet and intermingle.

Nepalese

Dawn rises over a Himalayan
village near Katmandu. Mount
Everest is one of the 23
snow-covered summits
in the world's highest range.

Nepalese farmers work closely
together irrespec.ive of caste
but rigidly observe many
distinctions dividing castes —
from Brahman to untouchables.

Compact villages like this
are rare in Nepal. Most
homesteads are liberally
scattered throughout the
hill-slopes and valleys.

established by immigrant Rajput in the hills of western Nepal survived for several centuries, and in 1768 one of the local rulers, the Raja of Gorkha, laid the foundation of the state of Nepal in its present form. It was only after the unification of the country under the royal house of Gorkha that Nepali became the *lingua franca* of the whole of Nepal. Brahman and Chetri, originally concentrated in the western part of the country, then also spread over most of the eastern districts. But even today more than half of all Brahman and Chetri live in the western hills, where they represent about 80 per cent of the population. In the lowlands of the Terai they are in a minority. While their political dominance has enabled them to impose many of their practices and religious beliefs on neighbors of different ethnic stock, the nature of the land has compelled them to adapt to local styles of dress and diet.

Throughout the middle-ranges, where most Brahman and Chetri have settled, they generally live in two-storeyed houses, built of stone or mud-brick and roofed with either thatch or slates. Only in the arid zones of the Jumla and Humla regions do they construct houses with flat roofs like those of the adjoining districts of Tibet. In most of their settlements their homesteads are widely scattered over hill-slopes and valleys. Only a few Brahman and Chetri maintain themselves by priestly work and many live little differently from other hill farmers. High status in the caste hierarchy does not necessarily mean a man is wealthy and many Brahman and Chetri peasants are no wealthier than their neighbors of lower rank. On fields carved out of hillsides or spread out in broad valleys they grow rice, wheat, barley and various millets, tilling the soil with a wooden plow drawn by oxen or buffalo. The rest of the farm equipment is equally primitive, and throughout the hills there is no wheeled traffic. Everything is carried on men's backs or occasionally by pack-animals. A very different situation prevails in the Terai, the extension of the Gangetic plains. There people similar to their neighbors in Bihar and Uttar Pradesh have made considerable progress, modernizing farming and establishing industrial enterprises.

In Katmandu and several other towns members of the high Hindu castes also engage in trade and are employed in government service. Most of the officers of Nepal's army are drawn from the ranks of Chetri and Thakuri, while Brahman predominate in teaching and the professions. Traditionally Nepali Hindus are extremely conservative. They insist on the rigid observation of caste rules; their supreme preoccupation is the avoidance of ritual pollution and of any action which might adversely affect their social status. Yet the high Hindu castes do not object to intercaste marriages as much as their Indian counterparts, and it is not unusual for Brahman to conclude formal marriages with Chetri girls.

91

Gracing the Katmandu valley are temples erected by Newar kings who patronized the arts and endowed both Hindu and Buddhist places of worship.

Nepalese

Near the base of Everest the gods of the Snowy Range are worshipped for three days and nights with music and chanting in the *Mani Rindu* festival.

92

Many Nepalese make long pilgrimages to Gokrana to pray and sacrifice to their deceased ancestors in the 'Fathers' Day' Festival.

At Pashipati, a Hindu temple 3 miles from Katmandu, a man is cremated in a traditional Hindu funeral ceremony.

Both Brahman and Chetri girls are usually married at an early age, and a first marriage is generally negotiated with the help of intermediaries. The elaborate wedding ritual extends over at least four days, and the rites and feasting are spread over the homesteads of both groom's and bride's parents. The bride receives from her parents a dowry of clothes, utensils and ornaments, and from the bridegroom presents of jewels and clothes. After the wedding the bride normally enters the house of her husband's parents.

The families of all high Hindu castes, Brahman, Thakuri and Chetri alike, are strictly patriarchal. All those living under the same roof – a man and his wife, or wives, his unmarried children and perhaps his married sons and grandchildren – are subject to the father's authority and expected to give him what they earn. In return their legitimate needs are met out of the family's common purse. Among peasant class Chetri married sons often separate from their father's household once they have children of their own, but among higher caste people there is a strong tendency to keep the family united until after the father's death.

There is no Nepali-speaking caste of true middle status. The Twice-born castes of Brahman, Thakuri and Chetri rank high above all communities, while the artisan caste such as cobblers, blacksmiths and tailors are untouchables and stand at the bottom of the social scale. It is such Tibeto-Burman speaking groups as Newar, Magar, Gurung and Tamang, who form the middle stratum of Nepalese society.

While the observance of untouchability has never assumed the extreme forms of discrimination current in some parts of India, members of the untouchable artisan castes are nevertheless excluded from most social contacts. They may not enter any part of a touchable's house and no person of clean caste will accept any type of cooked food or even water from the hands of an untouchable. Sexual intercourse and sharing a meal with an untouchable are among the gravest offenses which a member of a clean caste can commit, and as a consequence he would be excommunicated. Yet at harvest and planting time caste Hindus may work side by side with untouchable laborers.

Apart from the Chetri, who constitute the upper stratum of the peasantry of the hill-regions, there are Chetri families of great wealth and influence who live in Katmandu in a very different life-style. The most prominent of these families are the Ranas, who for nearly a century provided the hereditary prime ministers of Nepal, and regularly intermarried with the royal family.

Distinct from the politically dominant Nepali-speakers are the Newar of Katmandu valley and some of the market towns of the hill-regions. They speak a Tibeto-Burman language and form a closely knit, inward looking society. Theirs is basically an urban civilization, and even the expert tillers of the rich soil of the Nepal valley live side by side with craftsmen and merchants in compact towns with brick-built houses, several storeys high, standing in narrow streets and lanes. The Newar's artistic achievements surpass those of all other people in Nepal, and their business acumen and trading skills were largely responsible for Nepal's wealth and cultural afflorescence in medieval times. The three towns of Katmandu, Patan and Bhadgaon were built by Newar who ruled the valley until its conquest by the Raja of Gorkha. Racially the Newar are an amalgam of mongoloid and caucasian elements, but socially they present a homogeneous community averse to inter-marriage with other ethnic groups.

As early as the 7th century AD the Newar towns were renowned as centers of Buddhist learning. Accounts from Chinese travelers speak of thousands of celibate monks inhabiting the monasteries of Patan. Indian and Tibetan Buddhists met there for scholarly intercourse, and the great sanctuaries of Swayambuneth and Budhnath, still existing in all their ancient glory, have throughout the ages, attracted crowds of pilgrims from Tibet and the neighboring Himalayan regions.

Buddhism and Hinduism coexisted in the Newar towns, and in medieval times tantric influences began to dominate both religion and art. An emphasis on the mystic, the esoteric and the female principle brought about a change in the ascetic ideals of the monastic communities. The cult of the mother-goddess and the ritual use of blood sacrifices was incorporated into both Hindu and Buddhist practices. The two religions, sharing the belief in the efficacy of magical spells and secret rituals, became inextricably intertwined. The majority of the temples gracing the Katmandu valley were erected in the time of the last Newar dynasty. Grouped in an incomparable array in front of the royal palaces the temples are of varied architectural design, including the characteristic tiered pagoda roof.

According to Hindu principles the orders of celibate monks gave way to a hereditary priesthood and the buildings of the old monasteries became the residence of married priests, who today form the highest stratum of a caste-society with the full range of status-groups typical of Hindu societies, but complicated by vertical division into Hindu and Buddhist groups. Unlike those Buddhist populations which conform to the pattern of Tibetan lamaism, the Buddhist Newar are no less bound by caste-rules and pollution fears than their Hindu compatriots.

In their attitudes to marriage, however, Newar differ greatly from the Nepali-speaking castes. To the Newar marriage is not a sacred and indissoluble union, but an association which either party can terminate at will. Between the ages of seven and nine a Newar girl is symbolically married to a *bel*-fruit, and after this rite she is regarded as a married woman. According to Newar belief a proper marriage rite can be performed only once in a life-time, and all subsequent marriages are devoid of 93

Nepalese

Under the banners worshippers
of Kali, fang-toothed Hindu
goddess of death, assemble
the animals before sacrificing
them to her.

Before the actual sacrifice
citizens and soldiers display
their swords as they pledge
to follow the religion and
protect their country.

any sacred character, and can be easily dissolved.

For centuries, while first Newars and later Thakuri and Chetri have been the main actors on the political stage, tribal people inhabiting large areas of Nepal were seldom in the forefront of historic events. Yet these tribal groups, Gurung and Magar in the west, Tamang, Rai and Limbu in the east, form the backbone of the peasantry in many hill-regions and number well over 1·5 million. With few exceptions they speak Tibeto-Burman languages and are of a mongoloid physical type. Renowned for their hardiness and courage they provide most of the recruits for the Gurkha regiments of the British army, and many still serve in the Indian forces. Modern education and the system of basic democracy has enabled some sections of these communities to rise to prominent positions in politics and the administration, but the people in the hill-villages persist largely in their traditional way of life as farmers. They live in attractive, solidly built houses, which in the case of the Gurung stand in compact clusters, with stone terraces and long flights of stone steps, and occupy spurs or hilltops, high above the terraced fields. Traditionally Gurung breed sheep and move during part of the year with their flocks

94 Nepalese

Special swords are painted,
sanctified, then used to kill
the animal with a single blow.
All over Nepal hundreds of
goats are sacrificed this way.

During the women's festival at Pashupatinat, wives don their red wedding dresses and pray to the gods for happiness in marriage.

from pasture to pasture.

It is these regions of high altitude which culturally and ethnically form part of the Tibetan sphere. Bhotia communities, such as the Sherpa of Nepal, subsist there by agriculture, cattle-breeding and trans-Himalayan trade. In the highest inhabited valleys, where villages are between 11,000 and 14,000 feet above sea level, only barley, buckwheat and potatoes can be grown, and yak and cow cross-breeds are the main domestic animals. For many years trade with Tibet has been an important pillar of the economy of these Bhotia people. The mobility forced upon Sherpa husbandmen by the climate and the land has led to a proliferation of dwellings, each inhabited at certain times of the year and adapted to specific uses. As well as the main villages, where houses are spacious and furnished with a variety of valuable possessions, most Sherpa have subsidiary settlements near their high pastures where they spend most of the summer, and winter settlements in deep valleys.

The family system of the Bhotia also shows features not found among other ethnic groups in Nepal. They prefer polyandry – the marriage of one woman with several men, usually brothers – which prevents the fragmentation of estates by keeping several brothers in one household, and limits the number of their children.

Some Bhotia of western Nepal still travel with caravans of yak and carrier-sheep to Tibet where they barter Nepalese grain for salt and wool. But since the Chinese take-over of Tibet, this trade has steadily declined. The Sherpa of the Mount Everest region have been able to reorientate their economy towards the growing tourist industry, but for other high-altitude dwellers dependent on trans-Himalayan trade the outlook is far less favorable.

Contact between the northern border people of Nepal and the inhabitants of the neighboring districts of Tibet used to extend also to the religious sphere. Numerous Buddhist monasteries and nunneries had been established on the model of Tibetan institutions and, until the suppression of Buddhism by the Chinese, monks and nuns from Nepal regularly crossed the Himalayas to receive instruction and ordination in Tibet.

Today whole communities of Tibetan monks and nuns have sought refuge in Nepal and recreated there the monasteries from which they were expelled by the Chinese army. Nepal, together with Sikkim and Bhutan, is the last home of Mahayana Buddhism in its lamaistic form. At the same time it is the only surviving Hindu kingdom in the modern world. Hinduism enjoys the patronage of the politically dominant class and of the king, who is traditionally regarded as a reincarnation of Vishnu. And the religious tolerance which has always been characteristic of the Nepalese allows the peaceful coexistence of the two religions. Their interaction created the complex civilization of the Nepal valley where Hindus and Buddhists still worship at each other's shrines.

Village in south China

In the village of Sheung Shui mourners burn a paper chair for the dead woman to use in the afterworld. Her son performs the ceremony.

The village of Sheung Shui lies in the northwestern corner of the New Territories of Hong Kong, an area leased by Britain from China in 1898 for 99 years. It has a population of some 5,000 people. Well over 3,000 of these people all bear the same surname – Liao – and are the direct descendants, plus wives and children, of one common ancestor. Sheung Shui is in fact a lineage village.

The founder of the lineage, Liao Chung-chieh, first came to the area over 600 years ago. There he married and had one son. The son had three sons and so the group continued to grow over the generations. The village was walled and moated in the mid-17th century, but soon was outgrown by the lineage, which spilled over into the seven other hamlets which together now make up the village. Some 1,000 acres of land are owned by the villagers, most of it land of the best quality, and most of it in a wide belt around the village.

Like other Chinese villages Sheung Shui has its full complement of temples, earth gods, tree gods, spirit mediums, Taoist priests and so on, but it has also a number of ancestral halls and shrines which other villages do not have.

Under the lineage system families divide their private inheritances equally and members set up separate households. At the same time a proportion of the land to be inherited is kept back as communal land and held in trust for all descendants of the deceased. In Sheung Shui there are some 25 acres of ancestral land of this kind held in trust for the descendants of Liao Chung-chieh. Every member of the lineage has an equal interest in that land, regardless of whether he himself has private land or not.

When the original village was founded it was divided into four quarters. Each quarter was occupied by the descendants of the four men who composed the fourth generation of the lineage. Thus close kin lived close together even within the lineage framework. In time these four groups came to be known as the North, East, South and West sections. The seven other hamlets reflect clearly the tendency for near relations to stay together, for most of them are occupied exclusively by one or other of the sections. The original walled village still shows the same kinship groupings as when it was founded.

The main purpose of the ancestral trust is to provide an income which can be used to pay the costs of the ceremonies of worship of the ancestor who forms the focus of trust interest and membership. Chung-chieh is the focus of the lineage trust, and the first call upon the trust income is to pay for his worship. Similarly his three grandsons are each the focus of a trust, the membership of which is composed of his descendants. But these are not the only trusts which exist in the lineage, for other ancestors of later generations have also been focused upon in this way, and altogether over 450 acres of land are held by these 150 other trusts. Each one is 97

Village in south China

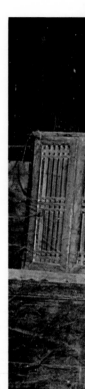

organized just like the lineage trust; but the later the generation of the ancestor focused upon, the smaller is the trust membership.

Ancestor worship does not use up all the income of some of the larger trusts, especially not of the lineage trust. The remainder of the income belongs, of course, to all trust members. In some cases it is shared out among them, but in others it is held as a communal purse from which to pay out for the general benefit of all trust members. Thus the extra trust income of the lineage is used to make roads, to dig wells, to build and service other works for the benefit of the lineage as a whole.

In the family, ancestor worship acts as the ritual sanction reinforcing the structure and unity of the group. In the lineage, it performs precisely the same functions. The tablet of Chung-chieh is kept in a large ancestral hall, where he is worshipped on the anniversary of his birth and also at the Spring Rites, one of the main ceremonies of the year. His is not the only tablet in the hall, for with it are many other tablets of early ancestors of the lineage. The ancestors are worshipped with food and drink mostly. Chief of the worshippers is the lineage headman. He is the oldest male of the senior surviving generation of the lineage – the 17th generation at present, in 1973. He it is who is technically the leader of the lineage, the only man who represents all the descendants of Chung-chieh. It is his main function to represent the lineage as a whole in worshipping its ancestors.

The lineage and segments also worship at the graves of the ancestors. Every year several hundred Liao men and children walk three or four miles in procession to the grave of Chung-chieh. Here the headman represents the lineage in worshipping, offering wine, incense, and vast amounts of food, including whole roast pigs. Afterwards everyone sits down beside the grave to eat a meal, which is prepared on the spot, wooden tubs being filled with the pork – a dozen or more pigs are killed and cooked for the occasion – mixed with pieces of squid, turnip and other vegetables.

The main lines of descent of the lineage are recorded in genealogies, which give personal details of the ancestors, including their dates of birth and death, the various names by which they were known during their lifetime, and their achievements. The history of the foundation of the lineage is also given, and links are traced back to ancestors as remote as 1,600 years ago. An important section of the genealogy lays down the rules for governing the group. Largely these rules are aimed at preserving the unity of the Liao, and they prescribe set punishments for offences against the lineage. Thus it is considered a grave offence for a man to become a monk, because this implies that he will be lost to the lineage and will not produce sons to keep the lineage strong. The punishment laid down is expulsion from the lineage and expunging the name from the genealogy.

While the leaders of the lineages were ideally headmen and elders, in practice these men had little power in the secular sphere. The men who really ran the lineage were the wealthy and influential. In Imperial Chinese times this often meant those who had passed the Civil Service examinations. They were able to capitalize on their literacy and wealth in dealing with the government. The Liao lineage like other lineages was wealthy enough and large enough to support scholars and in the course of its history had many successes in the examinations, some men holding office afterwards in the Imperial bureaucracy. The present day successors to the leadership are the wealthy businessmen who are wise in the ways of the very competitive world of Hong Kong. These leaders control even the religious sphere, for they have charge of the lineage trust income. They even take a considerable part in the worship of the lineage ancestors.

As Sheung Shui is both a lineage and a community the leaders have much to worry about. One major concern is with the renting out of the lineage trust lands and the management of the income. They have to organize annual ceremonies, maintain the ancestral hall and see that the elders get their due in gifts of pork at certain times of the year. At the same time, as village leaders they have to ensure good order in the village and that the community is provided with roads, wells, bridges, lavatories and schools. They have built an enormous modern secondary school since the 1950s. Over the years they have built dams and irrigation systems to feed the Liao land better. Also they organize a village watch to guard the crops and to give warning of floods, fire and thieves. Until this century the village watch was also the first line of defence in the event of attack by nearby lineages feuding with the Liao.

Walled and moated villages were necessary as protection, and the Liao lineage maintained an armory which included cannon, pikes and hand-guns. The old men still remember their fathers' tales of running battles and bitter enmities, and there is still comparatively little

These wooden cabinets
hold the spirit tablets
of important ancestors
of the Liao family lineage
in Sheung Shui.

A careless family
member may neglect to
burn the urn promptly.
The lid is then lost,
and the bones scattered.

The bones of the dead are
exhumed, cleaned and
ritually purified before
being rearranged in
burial urns.

intermarriage between the lineage and its immediate neighbors. Nowadays the hostility tends to take the form of economic competition both in business and in conspicuous display of lineage wealth.

The unity which lineage organization imposes makes it a most efficient form of village organization. By the 20th century the Liao territory had expanded to a point where on almost all sides it now meets the territories of other powerful lineages. The market town of Shek Wu Hui, which serves Sheung Shui and a dozen or so other villages, was built entirely on Liao land, and the market dues were collected by the lineage. Today some of the land has been sold and dues are much less important than before but the lineage still benefits quite heavily from the market.

From weaker villages lineages were able to buy young men as servants. These men were given homes and food and eventually wives. Their male children remained servants though daughters could be married out of servitude. By keeping these servants the lineages gained not only labor but prestige. In Sheung Shui still live the descendants of several such families, released from servitude in the 1930s.

Not only hereditary servants but also many other aspects of traditional life have disappeared from Sheung Shui. Formerly even the poorest members of the lineage were able to enjoy the reflected glory of their wealthy kin. They could also count on lineage support in any matter where they were in conflict with the outside world: it was a case of 'one for all and all for one'. But modern opportunities for individual advancement in the cities through education and business prowess have tended to break down the dependence of the lineage member and hence his loyalty to the group. Education, a sphere in which the lineage has excelled, has been contributing to the weakening of the lineage as men leave the village to find other work for which they are now qualified. The structure of the lineage remains, and it still has many useful functions, but it must ultimately become of little importance.

The Chinese

Frequent military parades
with much waving of red
banners and portraits of Mao
add festivity and excitement to
the Chinese working man's day.

Revolutionary China

Wherever there are people in China there are loudspeakers strung from trees and buildings, in parks and village halls. Loudspeakers broadcasting a constant stream of revolutionary music and political exhortations reach like tentacles into every corner of the vast country. And every morning all over China, in towns and villages, factories and schools, down mines and on trains, people pause in their activities. 'Comrades' the loudspeakers announce 'our great leader Chairman Mao teaches us to promote physical culture and build up people's health, heighten our vigilance, defend our motherland. Marking time on the spot . . . begin.' And with that, China's masses start their twice-daily keep-fit exercises. The exercises, which are followed by millions of people, are more than a simple campaign to keep the nation fit and healthy. They illustrate the remarkable discipline and regimentation that is the most outstanding single feature of the Chinese way of life.

Despite vast differences in geography and language throughout China there is a sense of national unity and identity. The communist leaders who came to power in 1949, inheriting a vastly underdeveloped nation debilitated by almost two decades of fighting, have achieved this through a powerful central authority, establishing party control down to the very lowest levels of the humblest peasant tilling the fields. The party plays a major role in the lives of everyone. Once a week people attend study classes or discussion groups, led by party cadres who outline the latest official thinking on a wide range of topics – from appeals to increase production to a visit by a foreign leader – and explain passages in the required reading of the classic works of communism by Mao, Marx, Engels and Lenin. The party structure works up from the level of a street committee in a town or a production brigade in a commune, through district, town, country and provincial revolutionary committee to the Central Committee which meets in Peking. Only a few million of China's 800 or so million people are actually members of the Communist Party, but they are the cadres (minor officials) and local leaders who guide and administer the brigades and committees.

A peasant in a remote commune may never have been to a city, let alone the capital. But he will have had a say in the selection of the local representative to the National People's Congress, a nationwide body whose several thousand delegates meet infrequently in Peking. He will also be able to question a party cadre if he does not understand how, for example, the government has invited President Nixon to visit China, after being told for years that the Americans were enemies, and he will be given rudimentary guidance to the change in official thinking that has brought this about. His access to news and information, however, is otherwise strictly controlled and principally limited to the loudspeakers.

It is through the media that the government makes its control virtually absolute. The radio – whether the pro-

The Chinese

Mao Tse-tung – the son of a peasant who brought revolution to China's millions in 1949. Since then his power was absolute.

Red flags wave and fireworks paint the Peking skies during a big parade. The flags and lights are reflected in the water under the arches.

Peking rail station is one of the few places in China where a foreigner may walk without being stared at. Peking is China's only cosmopolitan city.

vincial stations or the nationally-broadcast Radio Peking – the newspapers and the embryonic television service are all state-controlled and are a reliable, well-used means of shaping mass thinking along chosen lines. Like the quotation from Chairman Mao urging people to be healthy that precedes the keep-fit lessons, people are constantly exhorted to be unswervingly loyal to the Party, to 'unite to win still greater victories' or to 'learn from Tachai' – a model commune in the north that has broken many production records. The exhortations spill over from the radio and newspapers to vast posters and hoardings in the streets, on buildings and even fences along country roads. The huge, red Chinese characters, which often copy the spidery handwriting of Chairman Mao himself, usually bear a simple political inscription

In an open-air mime drama in support of North Vietnam long-nosed American pilots and Uncle Sam are caught up in the chains of the communists.

such as 'Workers of the world unite' – or quote a passage from Mao's *Thoughts*. These big character posters are everywhere, from the center of Peking's vast Tien An Men square to alongside the fishpond of a village in southern Kwangtung province, underlining the basic sameness of life everywhere.

This almost monotonous similarity of living standards, dress, ideas and social conditions, whether in the towns or countryside, has a strong unifying effect and has played a large part in the formation of a national identity. In China there is no jealousy from an underdeveloped west of the agriculturally and industrially richer east, as life in the two areas is essentially the same. Though there may have been a vast initial leveling-down by the communist leaders when they came to power, with the seizure of land, goods and property belonging to rich families, it is on the lines of an overall raising-up that they are aiming their dreams of a true socialist state.

With a nation as poor as China Mao and his colleagues had little alternative, without recourse to political ideology, to direct their efforts in the most basic way. They aimed to provide every single person with somewhere to live, enough food to eat, work to do and adequate clothes to wear. For all their drabness of dress and monotony of much of their labor, the vast bulk of China's masses are better off under the communists. Their diet may not be over-abundant or particularly varied, but carts no longer go round the streets of Shanghai each morning collecting the bodies of those who died in the night from cold and hunger – as they did in the 1930s when the city was under foreign rule and many of the great trading houses of the east made their fortunes. The monochrome blur of the drab blue-gray boiler suits that everyone wears make the peasant from the farm and his colleague in a factory hard to tell apart on a city street. But they both will have enough money in their pockets to buy a titbit from a corner stall or to pay the small charge at the bicycle park at the end of the street.

Peking's main shopping street, Wang Fu Ching, is always crowded. The road is jammed with a constant stream of cyclists all riding old-fashioned, identical, black Flying Pigeon bicycles. The crowds who jostle each other good-humoredly on the pavement, sip tea outside the East Wind market or queue for cheap but sturdy watches, are invariably dressed – men and women alike – in the same high-collared jackets, baggy pants and shapeless peaked caps. There is only one department store, one market and a couple of dozen other shops along Wang Fu Ching, but the goods in them are plentiful and varied by communist standards – and cheap by any standards. A meal in one of the several eating houses – a bowl of tasty noodles and a jug of draught beer – costs only a few pence. One yuan, the Chinese currency, worth 103

(Center) Students, workers and clerks meet outside working hours to learn to march. The soft-soled shoes they wear make for a noiseless parade.

about 50 US cents, will go a long way, from a cheap shoulder bag to a canvas cap or a couple of decorated mugs for drinking tea. A bowl of the hot, green tea that every Chinese consumes by the pint costs only two fen (100 fen to the yuan) from a cheery, whitecoated lady at the tea stall outside the market entrance.

Wages in China are low, but so is the cost of living. A factory worker or a farmer will earn about 60 yuan a month, but he pays only a nominal rent and virtually everybody, under strong official encouragement, has something in the bank. If a worker wants to draw from his savings he will approach the revolutionary committee of his production brigade or local street committee and explain why he wants the money. It may be to travel to see a sick relative, or buy a new bicycle, but in either case the final decision is taken by the committee. Nearly every Chinese owns a bicycle, a radio and a watch – and invariably buys them in that order when he has enough money. His clothes are mostly well-used and patched, but this is less a sign of hardship than due to natural thriftiness and the easy availability of repairs. A worker who tears his jacket will not take it home for his wife to mend, but stop off at the friendly neighborhood repair shop on the way. Little repair shops with their dozen or so sewing machines always whirring away are always handy, ready to sew a tear, put on a patch, replace a button and even stitch the letters of the national motto – 'serve the people' – on your workbag as you wait. The repair shops are well patronized for two reasons. Textiles are rationed on a basis designed to give complete new sets of clothes to each person each year. And in China a woman does not stay at home to tend the house, cook and look after her husband.

The emancipation sought by women's liberation groups in other parts of the world has already arrived in the People's Republic. The similarities between men and women extend to more than their distinctly utilitarian unisex clothes. Most women also go out to work and there are state-run nursery schools which look after children from a very early age, releasing the wives to return to their jobs in the shops, on the farms and in the factories. Women keep their own names after marriage, wear flat-heeled shoes and, at least for the public record, oppose wearing anything that might heighten their feminine allure. Married women do not wear wedding rings and they expect their husbands to share in the household chores. Arranged marriages, consulting astrologers for propitious wedding dates, and other old Chinese beliefs have long been abandoned.

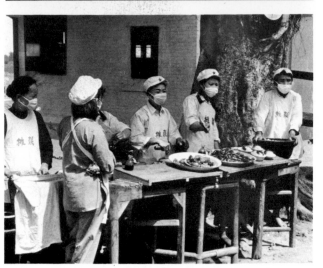

Young couples throughout the country are officially encouraged to put off marrying until they are at least 27 or 28 and then urged to keep the number of their children to two. After every marriage service, conducted by local street or revolutionary committee officials, every couple is given a 20 minute talk about birth control. According to official figures 85-90 per cent of all Chinese

Workers all over China, not only those who handle food, wear gauze masks as protection against colds and influenza.

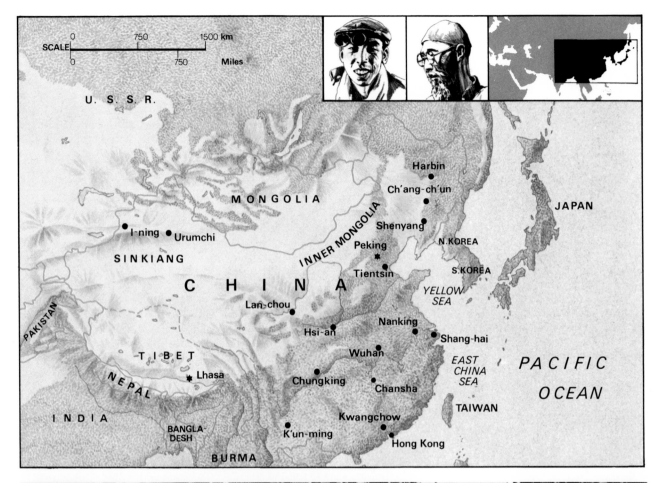

105

Peking's main shopping street,
Wang Fu Ching, is always
crowded with pedestrians and
cyclists who have come to buy
the cheap radios and watches.

couples practise some form of birth control and the effective introduction of family planning and contraception methods to millions of Chinese peasants is one of the Peking government's most remarkable achievements. The government launched successive campaigns to cut China's birth rate to under two per cent a year. Peasants were constantly exhorted to limit the size of their families to two or three children. Millions of 'barefoot doctors', women and young people given a six-month course in first-aid and methods of birth control, were trained and sent to virtually every village and factory. They keep medical records, dispense contraceptive pills, see that they are taken, and arrange for free abortions if necessary. Although the population is still increasing at an enormous rate – the Chinese account for nearly one-third of the world's population – officials say that without the campaign it would have been much higher.

The campaign to limit the number of people has also been beneficial in other ways, easing pressure on schools, housing and social services. Housing conditions are by western standards rudimentary. In the cities most people live in identical, sand-colored rows of workers' apartment blocks. The jumble of courtyards and low-roofed houses that made up the *hutungs* (alleyways) in the older parts of the cities are making way for more modern development.

In the villages most people still live in small, old houses, often built around the pig-sty where they keep the animals that are their most valuable possessions. But since the mid-1950s most communes have carried out campaigns to provide every household with a new house or at least an extension to their old home. About 80 per cent of China's vast population live in rural areas, planting their crops by hand and tilling the fields with plows drawn by water buffalo. But living standards are rising gradually. Mechanization is slowly being introduced. Even the poorest communes now boast a bicycle for nearly everyone, a sewing machine for almost every home, a push cart for every worker, a tractor for each production brigade and a truck for every commune. A modest record, but before 1949 most people were subsistence farmers renting small plots from large landowners. Now everyone shares in the profits made by a commune and each family has its own plot close by where it can keep animals or raise extra vegetables.

In the cities a large number of people still live in dormitories or share accommodation with other families. One of the prices that women have to pay for their emancipated role is the separation of families. Many people, whether they are married or not, are sent to do jobs in factories, in the People's Liberation Army or for the government, far away from their homes. A woman may be sent to work in Peking, for instance, leaving her husband and children in Shanghai. She may only see them two or three times a year, such as at the traditional Chinese reunion time of the lunar New Year holiday. The children will be looked after by relatives if possible or in state-run institutions.

To the vast majority of Chinese people hardships such as this are perfectly acceptable as a part of dedicated service to the state. Maoism has introduced into the Chinese way of life a strongly puritanical element that has made self-sacrifice, dedication and an unquestioning loyalty a common feature of the national character. It is this element in the Chinese character that is the most difficult for the foreigner to understand. It is largely responsible for the violent excesses of the Cultural Revolution, for example, and the unquestioning acceptance of what may be quite diametrically opposed policies or decisions; and the ostensible willingness with which desk-bound officials go to the countryside each year for a mandatory month-long stint of manual labor and 'learning from the masses'.

The tremendous, genuine enthusiasm for the cause that is apparent everywhere has brought a widespread belief in the infallibility of the teachings of Chairman Mao. And it has brought the government of the country generally up to a surprisingly high, and by Chinese standards sophisticated, level. A Chinese cadre when asked why something is done in a particular way, will answer 'It is the regulation.' To him there is no need to question further.

It is also this particular element that has dominated China's relations with foreign countries. On the occasions when the People's Republic has emerged from its shell of isolation contacts with the outside world have been eagerly sought and foreigners welcomed with unstinted hospitality. But when ties have slumped to a low ebb, as in the 1960s, foreign ways have been bitterly denounced and official dicta over-zealously translated by the party faithful into attacks on foreign property and foreigners themselves.

That such an attitude should have occasionally manifested itself is not surprising. For centuries the Chinese regarded their nation as the Middle Kingdom between Heaven and Earth lacking nothing and outside of which all was barbaric. Then for much of the 19th and the first half of the 20th century, China was attacked, exploited, plundered and economically raped by foreign powers. For more than two decades after the communists took power, the industrial and military might of the United States attempted to confine China behind a bamboo curtain as it feared that a tide of communism would, through sheer weight of numbers, sweep the world. It was only with the end of America's containment policy with the admission of China to a seat at the United Nations and with China's general re-emergence into international affairs in the early 1970s that foreigners were once again allowed into the country in increasing numbers and welcomed with open arms.

But for the average Chinese a foreigner is for the most

Shanghai (population nearly 7 million) is China's main port and industrial center, second only to Peking in cultural and educational facilities.

Most Chinese live within cycling distance from their work. This industrial area is in a suburb of Peking.

(Center) Workers at the steel plant in Ansnan know that their work is vital if the new China is to become fully self-supporting.

The bicycle is China's main means of transportation, and almost every Chinese has one. It can be used to carry freight as well as passengers.

Marching is a favorite pastime, practised from an early age. Members of the youth group 'Pioneers' parade with wooden guns.

The Chinese

The sons of the half-starved coolies of yesterday now support themselves making coke in a factory in the new eastern suburb of Peking.

part still an object of curiosity and, except for the blasé populace of Peking, where the diplomatic missions are situated, attracts large crowds wherever he goes. In virtually every town and city, crowds muster round to get a glimpse of visitors. As he strolls, the visitor may well get stopped by a worker or peasant anxious to practise his few phrases of English – like 'Long live Chairman Mao' – which he has learned from language lessons on the radio. Language lessons, particularly in English, are very popular among China's knowledge-hungry masses. Every child now goes to school, at least between the ages of 7 and 14. But China is still desperately short of higher education establishments, for which selection is as much a matter of correct political attitude as of intellectual ability.

The Cultural Revolution of 1966-69, which masked a bitterly divisive, topmost-level power struggle under the guise of instilling a fresh revolutionary fervor into the nation's youth, also wrought vast changes to the country's cultural life. Mao's wife, Chiang Ching, set out to re-model all art, literature, theater, opera, ballet and music along proletarian lines and, in so doing, almost single-handedly turned China's centuries-old culture into a vehicle for politics and ideology. A handful of ballets and operas, all praising the role of the masses and China's communist revolution, emerged and came to be virtually the only acceptable entertainment. China's masses hear and see these works almost endlessly, with no apparent reduction in their boundless enjoyment of the exploits of *The White-haired Girl* or *The Red Detachment of Women*. For most people, a film of a revolutionary opera or ballet is the only entertainment available, apart from a stroll in a people's park or some kind of sport such as table tennis.

Life in China today is essentially a simple affair led by proud, happy, healthy, normal people who are slowly becoming better known by the rest of the world and no longer feared as an ominous teeming mass of millions. Chinese society today above all owes virtually everything to one man, the leader of the Communist Party, Chair-

man Mao Tse-tung. Mao overturned the established society in pursuit of revolutionary ideals. He humbled the rich and powerful, and raised up the soldiers, workers and peasants as the models on which the country was to be based. He sent millions of students, intellectuals and officials down to the countryside to learn from the humble farmer, ending any form of meritocracy and replacing it with the selfless man who works untiringly for the good of his fellows and for the People's China.

The China that his policies have brought about may be a drabber place today than it once was. It is certainly a very different place from the rest of the world. Whether the Chairman's dream of pure socialism through the selfless man becomes a lasting and noble lesson for us all will take a long time yet to be seen.

The tortuous mountain passes and turbulent gorges of the Yangtze make it one of the world's most treacherous rivers.

(Above) Pulling on their oars, men hasten to get their junk past the rapids. The Yangtze is feared for its sudden floods and savage currents.

Men haul a group of boats
through the Hsin rapids on the
Yangtze. The headman in black
directs them and cracks jokes
to keep up their spirits.

A hydraulic press contributes its 12,000 tons worth of power to the People's Revolution in a Shanghai factory.

Rural traditions

In Chinese culture the city has had a part to play, but it has never developed into quite the same important focus of social life as it did in Europe. Chinese social norms grew up in the countryside and the city was something of an anomaly, which did not fit easily into the Chinese patterns of government or social organization. Cities had such small roles partly because most people lived in the country; as late as the 1920s, at a very conservative estimate, at least 70 per cent of the population of China lived and worked in the countryside. The figure has probably not changed even today. It is on the recent historical background of the village and the market town that our attention must focus to understand something of the lives of the majority of Chinese today.

Chinese villages are not difficult to find, as a 16th century Italian traveler discovered: 'of villages and hamlets (some of them containing a thousand households) the number is infinite; for the country is so covered with habitations, that all China seemeth but as one town'. Closer inspection would reveal that the villages were much more separate than that. A village was almost invariably a densely packed settlement surrounded by the fields which it owned and farmed. Each village tended to be doubly insulated, by its own, and its neighbors' lands. Each village was a cell within which the individual played out his life. Within it was a smaller and more important cell, the family.

Chinese political philosophers ascribed to the family a major role in the organization of society, and this formal recognition of a phenomenon which was without doubt apparent long before the school of Confucius adopted it in the 5th century BC did much to perpetuate and strengthen the family's power. Family organization was basically patrilineal: surnames, inheritance and title all descended from father to son. The family was a continuing organic unit, kept alive by its individual members. The family was more important than the individual. The individual's desires were subordinated to those of the family group. The male role was exalted over the female role and the role of the old was exalted over that of the

An actor makes up for one of the 'proletarian operas' devised by Chiang Ching, Mao's wife, who has remodeled Chinese art and literature.

China's centuries-old culture has been turned into a vehicle for politics and ideology. The 'People's Dancers' perform a proletarian dance.

In Lungmen 8th century
Buddhist grottos which
were once centers for religious
pilgrimage are visited today
for their historical interest.

young. Both these principles were carried over into society as a whole, so that the superiority of the senior to the junior generation, of age to youth, and of male to female was universally recognized.

Probably most Chinese families were simple families of father, mother and unmarried children. As only a son could carry on the family line sons were desired far more than daughters. If a family could not produce a son it would often adopt one. In a rich, son-less family the husband might take one or more concubines, for failure to produce children or sons was assumed to be the woman's fault. A concubine, it was hoped, could make up for the wife's inadequacy, and their sons had the same rights in the family as the wife's sons. All sons shared

equally in their father's estate. Daughters were not allowed to inherit property, nor could succession pass through them. Girls meant hardship for poor families, and female infanticide was quite common in times of famine or disorder. Selling female babies was the more usual answer to unwanted births. Girls were sold as servants or into prostitution in the cities.

For the first month of his life a child was kept secluded with his mother, protected from strangers behind doors guarded by good luck talismans. When the child was 30 days old he was considered to have taken a firm hold on life. A Full Month Feast was held at which he was given a name. His surname of course was handed down from his father, and his personal name too was sometimes 11

Near the North Vietnamese
border, soldiers return from a
day's building work. On the
blackboard they carry a
quotation from Mao.

Each year, desk-bound Chinese
officials go to the country for
a mandatory month-long stint
of manual labor with the aim of
'learning from the masses'.

(Bottom) Students and
soldiers, like clerks, are
made to taste the life
of the Chinese peasant
on the communal farms.

predetermined. It frequently happened that all the sons
in one generation, and sometimes even the daughters,
had one common element, decided many generations in
advance, in their personal names.

Although the birth of a son was a joyous occasion his
birthday was rarely celebrated. As the individual's progress through life was not of general concern everybody's
birthday was celebrated on the same day, the seventh
day of the lunar calendar new year. A child's progress
through the years was not marked by birthdays but by
his gradual assumption of more mature roles. Boys were
allowed a great deal of freedom until they were strong
enough to help in the fields or perhaps attend school.
Girls started helping with the domestic chores at a very
tender age. Before the mid-20th century girls were
seldom given an education. Their entire training was
directed towards a restricted life at home. A young girl's
feet were bound so that her growing bones broke and
became distorted and her feet remained small – for two
reasons. Her bound crippled feet made her sexually
attractive to men, who were excited both by her painful
gait and by the symbolism of exclusive feminity that
binding feet implied (like the preservation of a white skin
in western society). It also kept her relatively immobile
and therefore more firmly bound to her home.

No two people who had the same surname were
allowed to marry – although there were areas where this
rule was not acknowledged, or where it had been relaxed
because of the predominance of a certain surname among
the population. The age at which couples became betrothed was not uniformly laid down. Sometimes two
pairs of expectant parents would agree to betroth their
children to each other should the child each couple was
expecting turn out to be a boy and a girl. And in some
parts of China it was normal for young couples to be
betrothed when they were four or five years old.

In any case the couple seldom had any say in the choice
of their spouses. It was the families of the two people
who arranged the match, usually through the services of
a match-maker. The bride and groom might not even

The Grand Canal linking the
Yellow and Yangtze rivers was
completed in the 7th century.
The mighty waterways serve
the modern China too.

know of their impending marriage until it was practically upon them. As the bride moved into the home of her husband what the man's family looked for was a hardworking, submissive girl who would, without disrupting their household, add to its work force. Both families hoped for some advantage from the match. At betrothal gifts were exchanged, oracular advice on the harmony of the times of birth of the couple was taken and the payment in cash or kind which the groom's family would make to the bride's family was agreed. This 'bride-price' was a cause of much haggling – all carried on through the match-maker – which, once it was settled, had to be paid before the date of the wedding.

The wedding ceremony itself was not complex. A marriage party of match-maker, flag-bearer, musicians and friends of the groom (but not necessarily the groom himself) went in procession to the bride's house. The bride took a tearful farewell of her family and was carried weeping back to the groom's home, where she was confronted for the first time with her spouse and her new relations. She was expected to remain calm and undemonstrative while they scrutinized her and subjected her to frank remarks about her looks and possibilities. Together she and the groom worshipped his ancestors, and made obeisances to his father and mother, and to all the other senior members of the groom's

family in turn. She would meekly offer them tea, and in return older people would give her packets of 'lucky money'. Consummation of the match would be delayed until late at night to allow plenty of time for the custom of 'teasing the bride', by which the groom's friends tried to embarrass the couple and to draw an unseemly reaction from her.

The bride was expected to adapt quickly, and humbly, to the ways of her new home in which her position was of servitude to her husband and his family. She was not expected to feel or show affection towards her husband – she had after all only just met him – and the couple were often expected to ignore each other in company. Her status as wife was not really firm until she had borne a son and so ensured the continuation of the family. A woman could be divorced for *1* barrenness, *2* wanton conduct, *3* neglect of parents-in-law, *4* garrulousness, *5* theft, *6* jealousy and ill-will, *7* incurable disease. She could not be divorced if *1* she had kept three years mourning for either of her parents-in-law, *2* her husband's family became wealthy after she married into it, *3* she had no home to return to. Despite the ease of divorce implicit in these conditions, it was in fact almost unknown. A man could not be divorced by his wife.

A married woman lost all rights in the family in which she had been born and adopted her husband's surname 113

The Chinese

Women's liberation already exists in China: most women work outside their homes, often in another city. Children are cared for in communal nurseries.

Porters carry geese through Nanking. Once the seat of the Nationalist government, later sacked by the Japanese, it is now a quiet provincial town.

(Center) For centuries Honan was subject to a tragic cycle of famine and flood. Now there is enough food and women can sell bread in the market.

– which was often prefixed to her own – his fortunes and his ancestors. Her domestic services and her progeny were the property of her husband's family. She even lost her personal name, which could be regarded as a symbol of her individuality, for she was usually known after marriage as 'Mrs X' or 'née Y' or 'Z's mother'.

The simple family – of husband, wife and unmarried children – was the commonest form of family, but quite often the stem family, the husband and wife, lived with the surviving parents or parent of the husband especially in the early years of their marriage. Then the wife was just as subject to her parents-in-law as she was to her husband. Indeed, she was expected to owe stronger allegiance to them than to her husband. The husband's mother, jealous that her son's interest had been distracted and finding herself in clear authority over a relatively defenseless person for the first time in her life, often treated her daughter-in-law harshly. The girl was socially prohibited not only from returning this treatment, but even from complaining against it.

The division of labor at home between husband and wife was clear. The home was exclusively the wife's province. In the fields the husband might quite frequently need his wife's help particularly at busy times such as planting, weeding and harvesting. The poorest farming families did not bind women's feet as the woman's freedom to work was essential for survival.

The husband in due course became head of the family and, nominally at least, the most important member of the family. It was at this stage of life that he might begin to have his birthday anniversary celebrated with a small feast. His importance as family head was bolstered by his control of the family finances. All the family income passed through his hands to be shared among the family as he saw fit. As a man aged his physical strength declined and he might be forced to cede some of his authority to his grown son who gradually took over his work. In the home the mother, however, could remain well in command. As the couple aged the woman came more into her own, although in theory she was always

114

Sons of peasants and factory hands feel fortunate to be students even under the austere and strict conditions of Chinese dormitories.

subservient to her husband.

Old people who could see around them in the house not only a son, his wife and children, but several married sons with their families, and perhaps even great-grand-sons too, were the most fortunate. Indeed an extended family of this kind was in many ways considered the ideal Chinese family. In practice, though, it was difficult to attain. Building up such a large family group demanded considerable wealth, and to hold it together required unusual harmony of personalities.

Death was attended by most elaborate ceremony. Funerals were as expensive as a family could afford, and anxiety to bury a parent with full honors often resulted in years of subsequent debt for surviving relations. Mourning for parents was prescribed by law. A father or mother were due 27 months' deepest mourning, abstinence from eating meat, from sexual relations and from either work or entertainment. It was impossible of course for the poor to give up work. But if an official failed to notify the death of a parent to the emperor and immediately resign from office he risked severe punishment. White was worn for mourning. Mourning costume and the duration of mourning varied according to the closeness of relationship with the deceased.

Ancestor worship was the most widespread and perhaps the deepest-held of Chinese religious beliefs. When a person died his soul went down to hell, where it was judged and held in an appropriate court for punishment and expiation of sin.

Belief in the soul was clearly heavily influenced by Buddhism, imported from India in the first century AD. The soul would ultimately be reborn into the world. But as a man had more than one part to his soul, there was a second part which remained with the corpse through the funeral service and into the grave. This soul could be worshipped for many years afterwards by the man's descendants. They expected that by worshipping it the soul was capable of bringing benefit to them, as the ancestor presumably had access to some form of divine power. Yet another part of a man's soul was enshrined in a wooden or paper tablet which was kept in the home. This soul was worshipped daily by the family, again in the expectation of supernatural aid.

Ancestor worship clearly reflected the organization of the family and gave a ritual sanction to its power structure. Only male children were fully-fledged, permanent members of the cult. This was because a woman's religious allegiance changed when she married, and she could worship only her husband's ancestors and not the ancestor of her natal family. When she died she could not, by the same token, be worshipped by anyone from her natal family, but only by her own sons and their families. So a woman had to marry and have sons if she was to establish herself in the afterworld. The unmarried, son-less woman had no-one to worship her. Her soul was condemned to a hungry, lonely period in hell followed by extinction. A childless woman could not logically become an ancestress. A woman without sons could not ritually become an ancestress. For ancestors were by definition of a superior generation to the living. Ancestors were worshipped as superiors. They helped to reinforce the idea that age was superior to youth in the living family.

The afterworld was considered somewhat similar to this one. The dead felt the same needs as the living. Worship took the form of providing the dead with what they required for their life in the afterworld. Housing, clothing, transport (including, recently, cars and air-craft), servants and money could all be offered to them in the form of paper replicas. These were translated into the real thing in the afterworld by burning them in this world. Real food, drink and tobacco were offered too: the ancestor extracted the essence of the offerings and his practical minded descendants afterwards consumed the remainder.

Mixed with ancestor worship were other religious beliefs. Many people worshipped a great variety of gods. As Buddhist beliefs had a major influence on Chinese thought there existed a large pantheon of gods some of whom were originally connected with Buddhism. The goddess Kuan Yin was one of the most popular. She originated as a boddhisattva – a being sufficiently advanced to enter nirvana, but who chooses to remain in the world of incarnation in order to save others. There were temples to Kuan Yin all over China. Other gods were mythical emperors, legendary heroes, and local men and women deified as a reward for outstanding deeds. There were also territorial gods who each guarded their own area of land: tree gods, water gods, rain gods, stove gods, grain gods and many others. Ghosts and evil spirits were rife and threatened the world at all times, so that they too had to be constantly guarded against and propitiated. In many cases the Chinese were rather sceptical of all these gods' powers, though not sceptical enough to stop worshipping them. The gods and ghosts, too, were fortunately not so clever as to avoid being tricked by the living. The Chinese built walls across the front of their doors because evil spirits, they said, could only fly in straight lines, and so were unable to fly round the ends of the walls and into the houses to cause trouble. Similarly the stove god, whose job it was to make an annual report to heaven on the doings of the household, was easily stopped from making a bad report by offerings of sticky cakes which seized up his jaws.

The ancestors were to the family what the gods were to the village. All members of a family were united in their descent from and worship of common ancestors. All members of a village worshipped the same deities who symbolized the unity of the settlement. The most common of these territorial deities were the earth gods, the guardians and supernatural overseers of land. There were greater and lesser earth gods, sometimes arranged in a hierarchy of importance, but always each one represented 115

Smiling at the sight of her newborn baby – this young mother has just had a painless delivery in which acupuncture was the only anaesthetic.

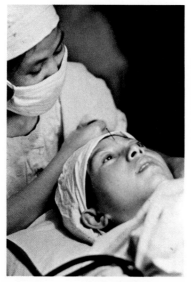

and watched over an area of land which was a recognizable social unit. The earth god presided over a village as a whole, or a ward of a village, or a temple precinct.

For many peasants the village, and perhaps the market town which served it, marked the limit of his normal social world. Within this small cell he lived, worked, worshipped, married and died, and an overall Chinese society can have meant little to him.

Organization of village affairs was usually in the hands of the most influential, wealthy families. Where a man had been successful in the Imperial Civil Service Examinations, he and his family would certainly be among the leaders of the community. It was most often the wealthy who were able to study and immense prestige was attached to those who had proven literary abilities. Old age too was much respected, and some villages were run by councils of elders. There were officially appointed village representatives, but often these men had little or no power or influence.

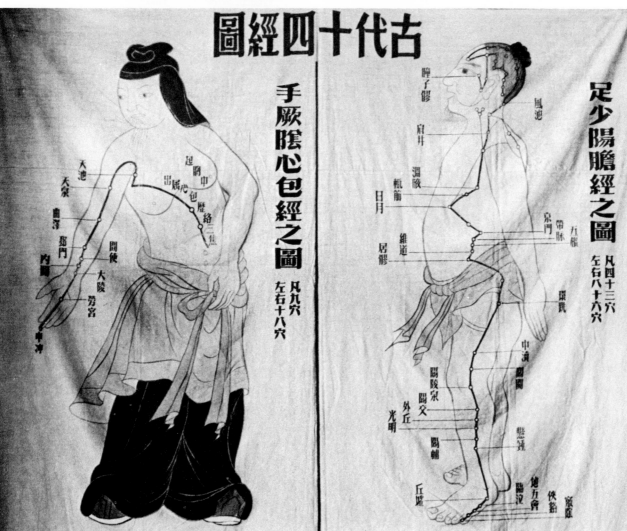

118

This 500 year old medical chart illustrates the points in which needles should be inserted for the cure or relief of various ailments.

Europe's idea of China is largely based on pictures painted in Kwangsi Province, where hills rise out of the mist beyond the River Kuei.

The Chinese produce their own tractors now, but within their social system man as yet faces little danger of being replaced by machines.

119

Some pre-revolutionary customs survive today in modified form: this old peasant, like a pre-revolutionary land-lord, is carried in a chair.

The Chinese

The Great Wall of China was
built of granite, filled in with
earth around 214 BC to keep
out the northern barbarians.
It is nearly 1,500 miles long.

Within the village or other local community the leaders, however appointed, would assume wide powers. When the state was weak they formed village guards to protect them from bandits, thieves and other evils. Even at the best of times crops, as well as lives and other property, needed watching, and this too was their responsibility to organize. They collected taxes for local public works such as irrigation channels, wells and roads. Internal order required them to arbitrate in disputes, and to punish or reward those whose actions were beneficial or harmful to the community. Punishments could be very severe, included capital punishment, and were often administered according to a well-accepted local scale of values. It was, for example, customary in some parts of China for adulterers to be punished by drowning. These powers were not officially sanctioned but, as resort to the legal system was officially discouraged and as the state was often too weak to manage full internal security, the local leaders found by default that it was necessary to substitute their own for imperial authority.

Land was the securest form of wealth. Owning land was the most important ambition of all. At times of dynastic weakness land-ownership tended to be concentrated in the hands of the few. Eventually rebellion or incursion would overthrow the dynasty, there would be

Political meetings are often
the only recreation Chinese
workers are offered after
their day's work. These Yanan
peasants seem to enjoy them.

(Bottom) Discovered in 1968,
these shrouds are made of over
2,000 pieces of jade stitched
with gold thread for a prince
and princess of the Han dynasty.

much slaughter, and often a massive redistribution of land. Decades of peace would allow the hoarders and the hard-working gradually to benefit by the land of the spendthrift, the idle and the unfortunate, and the inevitable concentration of land-ownership would again gradually take place.

By the mid-20th century a hundred years of ineffectual government, civil war, rebellion and military and economic invasion had given rise to just such a polarized situation. Western industrial models were examined for solutions to the economic problems but without success. The Chinese communist answer was radically different. The peasant and the land were China's strength. The worker and the factory could, initially at least, take second place. This emphasis readily appealed to the vast mass of the Chinese people, who flocked to the communist banner in their thousands. The communist victory of 1949 was followed by redistribution of land on an egalitarian basis.

Land reform was but the first step of the communist program. It was rapidly followed by movements to create co-operative labor groups, and finally to abolish private ownership of land altogether. The Chinese peasant now owns no land, although he usually has a small plot on which he can work alone and the fruits of which are at his disposal.

Another major reform was in the position of women. Arranged marriage, bride-price, concubinage and inequalities in divorce rights were abolished, clearing the way for a rise in women's status. Almost universally job opportunities are the same for both sexes.

The Chinese family has been much altered. All private landownership and the patrilineal system have been abolished. The possibility of forming an extended family has been removed. The stem family is not uncommon, for the necessity to care for the aged remains even if the authority of the aged is no longer respected. The simple family is still the norm.

The importance of ancestor worship, the religious sanction behind family strength and the age hierarchy have also been much reduced. They can now be regarded as having little more significance than the western approach to remembrance of the dead. All other religious beliefs have been branded as superstitions and their rituals discouraged.

Co-operative labor and the abolition of private land have turned the eyes of the peasant outward from self and and family to neighbor and comrade. At the same time the integration of villages into much larger economic and political groupings such as the commune has tended to break down the cell-like structure of Chinese society and some of the parochialism which accompanied it. The commune and its components are part of an administrative structure which brings state and peasant into a closer relationship than ever before. Leadership is vested not in the wealthy but in the politically orthodox.

The Chinese heritage

Street scene 1871: a soup
stall; a fortune-teller and
scribe, importuned by a
beggar priest; a barber; and
a turner selling spoons.

The last dynasty

In 1644 the Manchu swept into Peking, usurped the Dragon Throne of the Ming, and established a new dynasty in China – the Ta Ch'ing, or Great Pure. Following a tradition of China's conquerors, they succumbed to the wisdom, venerability, and effectiveness of China's ancient philosophy. They adopted Confucian institutions, including the absolute despotism of a sacred emperor, 'Son of Heaven', and the ceremonies and rituals which regulated every detail of the emperor's daily life.

Within the massive purple-stained walls of the Imperial City, courtyard led into courtyard, gateway through gateway, until the Forbidden City within was reached, and the emperor's scarlet and gold apartments, his decorative pavilions and ornamental gardens. The palace occupied a square kilometer, and constituted a miniature city in itself. To the west lay the so-called Sea Palaces, a sequence of exquisite buildings on three artificial lakes; to the south ran the Golden Water River, spanned by marble bridges; to the north rose Prospect Hill, a mound raised according to geomantic laws to ward off the inauspicious spirits of the north. Throughout the palace were scattered temples – to the Tutelary Gods, to the Imperial Ancestors – and immense Throne Halls, where, seated on carved mahogany, with lacquered screens and huge urns around him, the Son of Heaven heard the counsel of his ministers, crouched before him in the ultimate act of self abasement – the Three Knockings and the Nine Prostrations, the *kowtow*.

The Forbidden City was ablaze with color: the walls, columns, the carved brackets, rafters and joists of the wooden buildings were painted vermilion, scarlet, gold and peacock. The many curving roofs were covered with imperial yellow glazed tiles that gleamed when one viewed Peking from Prospect Hill above. The staircases and terraces of Yunnan marble imported by the Ming were chiseled with dragons and 'feng' birds, symbols of the male and female principles; auspicious emblems – bats, pomegranates, apples, peaches and lotus – were painted, carved, or embroidered all over the palace.

A sprawling bureaucracy supervised the Forbidden City. Under the Imperial Household Office were subsidiary departments: they guarded the vaults of gold and silver bullion, and the stores of furs, silk, tea, and porcelain. Other departments collected rents on Manchu property; others provided the meats and fruits for the emperor's sacrifices. There was one to organize the court's theater, another to run the kennels where the famous Pekingese dogs were bred; yet another was charged with maintaining the palace building and fabric. And attached to these were secondary boards: the palace stud, the imperial armory, the imperial buttery, the imperial weaving and dyeing office, as well as bureaux to take care of the emperor's boats, wardrobe, gardens, printing office, library, and silkworms.

But there was one major difference to this replica of an 123

The Chinese heritage

Tiny feet were considered
sexually attractive by the
Chinese. The ruling Manchu,
however, did not bind their
women's feet in childhood.

For nearly 1,000 years young
girls had their bones broken
and crushed to produce the
erotic 'lily feet' which also
kept them tied to the home.

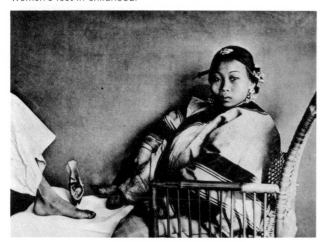

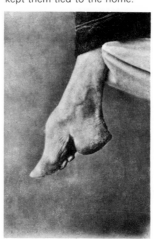

empire: it was entirely staffed by women and eunuchs.

The Son of Heaven lived alone in the Forbidden City, with 3,000 eunuchs, and, by the end of the Ch'ing dynasty, as many women. His relations and his ministers spent the day in the palace, but slept outside, in their own houses in Peking. Often he only saw other men in the most formal circumstances of an imperial audience. He was therefore, and particularly throughout his claustrophobic upbringing, exposed to the eunuchs' pernicious and enervating influence. The system did take its toll and eventually led to the corruption to which the Empress Dowager Tz'u-hsi was to give full rein from the 1860s to 1908.

In China, as in other polygamous countries, eunuchs had originated as the guardians of the emperor's harem – the guarantors of the chastity of his wives and concubines, and the consequent authenticity of the succession. Over the years inflation set in until the original point of the system was lost: under the Empress Dowager Tz'u-hsi, when there were either child emperors on the throne or one or two concubines only in the depleted harem, there were more eunuchs than ever in the Forbidden City.

Although a palace eunuch was paid a derisory sum plus daily rice, he was also entitled to a cut on all money that passed through his hands, and of the jewels, jade, silks

124

As in all societies which
require that their women be
wives, mothers and beauties,
Manchu women spent much
time on their appearance.

Hair was gathered up and
weightily decorated with
jewels shaped like flowers
and insects, with tassels of
pearl if the husband was rich.

The wives and daughters of the wealthy Peking official stand on the balcony while his eldest son has the place of honor at his side.

125

Sedan chairs were kept by rich mandarins and people of rank. Their wives had no other way of going out. They could not walk on bound feet.

Poorer people used the 'Shanghai cab'. The wheelbarrow was one of many things invented in China and later adopted by the west.

Prisoners kowtow before a Peking magistrate. The Manchu legal code demanded that the accused confess before they could be punished.

Criminals were savagely punished. These stocks were a mild punishment compared to starvation in a cage or beheading.

(Center) The Cangue or collar was another punishment, inflicted for minor offenses such as petty thieving.

and tribute of all kinds that were sent to the emperor in such quantities that pilfering went unnoticed. As eunuchs were allowed to leave the Forbidden City, provided they returned by sunset, many were able to establish their own houses in Peking from the splendid proceeds of the 'squeeze', as it was called. Occasionally they married, and adopted children to save face. However rich or influential, eunuchs were wholeheartedly despised. A common saying was 'he stinks like a eunuch: you get wind of him at 500 yards'.

The Chief Eunuch was chamberlain of the household and responsible for the army of gardeners, carpenters, cooks, cabinet-makers, painters, glaziers, tailors, laundrymen, scullions, cleaners and actors under him. He moved with the emperor, and often an official could only obtain access to the ruler by liberally greasing the chief eunuch's palm beforehand. Under the Empress Dowager Tz'u-hsi, her favourite Li Lien-ying was notorious for the ascendancy he exercised at court, and for his personal fortune.

In summer the emperor and his court fled the stifling dry heat of Peking for the cooler lakes and hills of the Summer Palace. K'ang-hsi, one of the greatest of the Ch'ing emperors, had begun building the Yuan Ming Yuan, the 'Round Bright Garden', in 1709, and since then each of his successors had added to the beauties of the palaces and the landscape, laying out the arbors and pavilions and gazebos, the rockeries, lakes, trees and paths in such a way that it seemed the wild, untouched charm of nature.

In 1860 the British, at the orders of Lord Elgin, their plenipotentiary, set fire to the palaces of the Yuan Ming Yuan and razed them to the ground. The sacrilege was intended to avenge the death of British and French prisoners of war. In fact it only set a seal on the Chinese opinion of the brute barbarians for, except for the many objects that had been looted by the British and French armies, nothing remained.

In the 1890s, the Empress Dowager, who had set her
126 heart on restoring the Emperor's honor by rebuilding his

Since time immemorial China has been plagued by revolts and rebellions. When they failed public executions were a common sight.

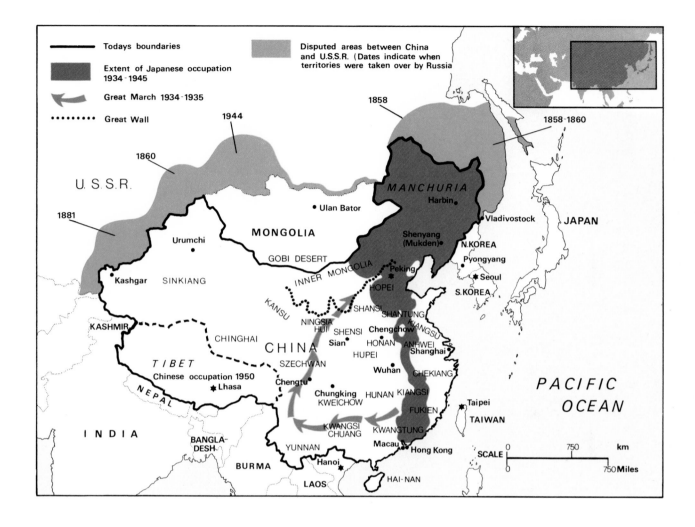

Legend:
- Todays boundaries
- Extent of Japanese occupation 1934-1945
- Great March 1934-1935
- Great Wall
- Disputed areas between China and U.S.S.R. (Dates indicate when territories were taken over by Russia)

palace, used her compliant brother-in-law, the Head of the Admiralty, to embezzle navy funds for the New Summer Palace. The continuous cycle of wars, rebellions, indemnities and inflation, as well as natural disasters that had tumbled on China since the first Opium Wars of 1839-42 never checked Tz'u-hsi's extravagance. On the shores of the K'un-ming lake, on the ruins of one of the former palaces, new temples and arbors and pavilions rose again. Rather bizarrely, Mississippi paddle steamers had caught the empress's fancy: she built one of white marble on the lake. It was, most people commented, the only boat built with the navy funds she had stolen.

The court rose at dawn. The morning audiences then took place in one of the Throne Rooms and, unless there was some crisis more overwhelming than the continual state of crisis in China during these years of decline, the business of government was over for the Empress that day. With her eunuchs and ladies about her, she then set out on one of her favorite meanderings through the palace gardens. In the full panoply of her embroidered robes, with her magnificent headdresses and raised jeweled shoes, under tasseled state parasols, with twelve musicians always in attendance and other retainers in dragon robes at her side, she must have presented a breathtaking sight of oriental splendor as she made her progress through the gardens. At various points she would stop to gaze at the view over the lake, or to sample some delicacy a eunuch would cook for her on a portable stove or produce from a lacquer picnic basket; or she would paint some scrolls with her handsome calligraphy.

The system of autocratic government that such a magnificent court reflected and bolstered was super-annuated; and Tz'u-hsi, who ruled China for the last 50 years of the Ch'ing dynasty, was herself a monstrous relic. For three years after her death in 1908, the Manchu staggered on; but in 1912 the child Emperor abdicated in favour of a Chinese Republic and in 1924 the court was finally expelled from the Forbidden City.

127

Tz'u-hsi, the despotic Dowager Empress, rose cunningly from a mere concubine to become China's ruler for nearly half a century.

(Below) The headless bodies of a band of Chinese pirates lie at the feet of the British officers who supervised the execution in Kowloon in 1897.

(Left) Three ministers in the government of the 1860s; a troubled time for China, faced with the problem of western expansion.

Culture

The history of the Chinese over the past 3,500 years has been of territorial expansion, of great cultural development, and of comparative isolation from the other major cultures of the world.

The earliest evidence of man's existence in China was discovered in the 1920s, when some of the remains of 'Peking Man' were dug up in the north of China. He is said to have lived about half a million years ago. But it is not until the neolithic period that we begin to have any considerable knowledge of how men lived. They appear to have inhabited much of north and central China, living in round earth-walled, thatched houses, grouped together in large settlements. They had acquired pottery-making techniques and had domesticated dogs, sheep, pigs and oxen. They practised a form of divination by cracking bone or shell with heat. By about 1500 BC they had discovered bronze and developed a system of writing with the oracle bones and shells, and a distinct culture.

To the north of China the terrain was unsuitable for agriculture. Harsh winds quickly stripped away the exposed soil once its grass cover was removed. So a particular kind of culture emerged there, a culture of pastoralists who tended their flocks of sheep and goats and relied on horses and camels. These people had neither a writing system nor a settled way of life. Chinese civilization came ultimately to despise the pastoralists as barbarian. It also feared them for their fierce restlessness. So in the north there was a natural geographical and human frontier – which was reinforced later by the 1,400 mile long Great Wall of China. This was built in the 3rd century BC and rebuilt by successive governments.

To the south, south-west and east there were not the same obstacles to expansion, and it was in these directions that the Chinese spread. Under the pressures of Chinese expansion the less-developed peoples of the south were either defeated and absorbed by the stronger culture, or confined to the high and agriculturally inferior lands

129

A remnant of The Ever Victorious Anglo-Chinese force who had been trained by European discipline and drill.

British exploitation of the
opium market led to the first
Anglo-Chinese war and the
first of many humiliating
defeats by western powers.

which the Chinese did not covet. Some islands of these non-Chinese peoples – Tai, Miao and Lolo – still remain.

The first great southward movements came during the shortlived but very efficient Ch'ing dynasty (221–206 BC) and the much more enduring Han dynasty (206 BC–220 AD). Though much of present-day China was nominally ruled from the north, the Chinese did not really control or settle the south until about a thousand years ago or even more recently. The highly productive double-cropping rice lands of the south quite early became an important source of food for the north and the economic center of China shifted south with the Chinese advance into these more fertile regions. China's immense canal systems were built largely to transport rice and also to enable the north to improve its control of sources. The process culminated in the early 7th century AD with the building of the arterial waterway, the Grand Canal, a project linking the Yellow River and the Yangtze.

China's political center did not move south in the same way. The greatest danger to the Chinese state was always posed by the barbarian tribes of the north. The capitals of China have always been in the north, where strong political control was essential. And the same pressures from the north have been responsible for great southward surges of people as they were ousted from their northern homelands by invaders.

The Chinese language appears to have developed in the northern region in one basic form with probably only relatively minor differences of dialect in different areas. Variations probably depended partly on political groupings as well as possibly even on social class. Present-day Chinese languages, however, are very different from each other and, although the vast majority are descended from a root language which was spoken at least as recently as 600 AD, in many cases mutually unintelligible. Doubtless the successive waves of population migration have had their effect, in some places tending to fossilize the language, in others altering it quickly as social conditions changed or through contact with other languages. The Chinese language developed five or six main branches each of which is divided into many dialects, some so different as to be almost separate languages.

Although he is a poor peasant, this village elder was accorded deference and respect as demanded by the Confucianist ethic.

The army of Sun Yat-sen, 'father of the Chinese Revolution' in 1923, during power struggles after the fall of the Manchu dynasty.

Certain features are common to all Chinese languages. Probably most marked is the fact that all of them are *tonal*; any one sound may be spoken with different pitch and voice-play to give different meanings. Modern Mandarin has four tones: a high level tone, a high rising tone, a low dipping tone and a high falling tone. The sound *cha*, for example, pronounced in each of the four tones would mean 'a fork', 'tea', 'to tread on', and 'to differ' respectively. Other Chinese languages have different numbers of tones. Cantonese, for example, is said to have a basic eight-tone pattern. All the languages are monosyllabic. Almost without exception all monosyllables are meaningful, but all make use of the device of adding monosyllable to monosyllable in order to produce compound words. Whereas words like *coalman* abound, there are no words like *trouble,* in which the separate syllables are meaningless. All languages have few sounds (Mandarin has only about 420 phonetically distinct syllables), and all have many homophones—in some cases scores of words which share the same sound and tone. Many features common in other languages do not

exist in the Chinese language. There are no irregular verbs, no gender, no number, no tense change in verbs, no declension, no conjugation, no mood, and no case.

The Chinese system of writing began as a pictographic system. The oldest discovered examples of pictographs, or picture characters, were carved on bone or shell, and recorded questions asked of the gods and the answers they gave when the piece of bone or shell was heated and cracked to obtain the oracle. The earliest known characters were already slightly stylized versions of the objects they were meant to represent. Thus 木 represented a tree, 果 fruit, 車 a chariot (two-wheeled and viewed from the top), 月 the moon, 日 the sun, 人 a man, 水 water, 羊 a sheep, and so on. Later these became refined and further stylized until in the first century AD a script emerged which squared off the rounded parts of the old characters, and which has remained to the present day. The above characters in standard form are written

木, 果, 車, 月, 日, 人, 水, 羊

As well as simple pictographs of this kind there were two other methods of forming characters. The first was to make complex pictures out of the accepted simple ones, often to represent an abstract idea rather than a physical object. Thus the sun and the moon put together made the character 明 to represent 'bright' or 'brightness'. A woman 女 and a child 子 put together made the character 好 meaning 'to love', a man leaning on a tree 休 meant 'to rest', and so on. The second method was to represent ideas without reference to other graphic 131

The Chinese heritage

Japanese troops march under the Chungeshan Gate after the capture of Wanking in the Sino-Japanese war which lasted from 1937 to 1945.

Until the 1940s travelers in Peking met palace eunuchs who earned their living telling tales of the court and its scandals.

elements, thus 一 , 二 and 三 were for 'one', 'two' and 'three', 上 and 下 for 'above' and 'below' and 中 for 'middle'.

The phonetic principle created the largest group of characters (90 per cent of all the tens of thousands which have been invented), forming characters with two elements of which the radical element indicated the category of word represented and the phonetic element indicated the sound of the word. Thus the radical element 木 'tree' appears in many of the words for objects made of wood, as well as in the characters for various kinds of tree. The character 松, for instance, means a 'pine tree'.

The second element 公 (*goong*) is a phonetic element and gives a clue to the pronunciation of the character 松, which is read *soong*.

The radical-phonetic method has been a fruitful generator of new characters, but the phonetic value of the method should not be over-estimated. Even in early times the phonetic elements were apparently in many

Communist success in 1949 owed much to peasants who supplied food to the army during the civil war against the Kuomintang.

(Below) After the Revolution thousands of peasant farmers were recruited for the army. China was at war a year later, against Korea.

cases only rough approximations. The characters 功, 紅, 扛 and 江 all have the same phonetic element 工 (*goong*), but are nowadays pronounced in Mandarin as *goong, hoong, gang* and *jiang* respectively.

There was one great advantage in a system of writing which was not too rigidly wedded to speech. The characters had to be learned as representations of ideas rather than of sounds, and they were thus meaningful without reference to the spoken word. This meant that as the Chinese language diversified, it was still possible for people to communicate, even when they could not understand each other in speech. Let us take for example the character 人 which means 'man'. Both a man from Peking in north China and a man from Canton in the south can understand that it means 'man', although the former would read it *ren* and the latter *yan*. (The Japanese use it to mean the same and read it *hito*!)

The written language became the great unifier of China, the vehicle which carried the culture which we recognize as Chinese. But as it was divorced from speech the grammar and vocabulary of written Chinese fossilized, and for many centuries this Classical Chinese was virtually a separate form of the language, useful in unifying China, but a huge obstacle which has only recently been removed to mass literacy.

In the 3,500 years of their recorded history the Chinese have discovered, invented and created much, bringing their civilization to high peaks of scientific and artistic achievement. Many of the basic inventions and discoveries upon which modern science has been built were first made by the Chinese, often long before they were adopted or independently discovered in Europe. They include, for example, the magnetic compass, gunpowder, the crank, the wheelbarrow, printing, silk, the rocket and porcelain. Chinese medicine developed in at least one unique direction with the science of acupuncture, the potential of which is perhaps only now beginning to be exploited. Chinese methods of deep-drilling for brine and natural gas, which date back to long before the time of Christ, were exported some two thousand years later to the oilfields of America. In the arts the Chinese carried painting and ceramics to great heights. They developed an idiosyncratic art form of calligraphy. They produced many different styles of prose, poetry and drama.

In natural resources of all kinds China was rich and self-sufficient. There was no lack of space for expansion within the bounds of China proper. And there was the insulating effect of the Chinese linguistic and writing systems, neither of which was related to any other major system. As a result the Chinese have always been markedly ethnocentric. What was foreign to Chinese culture tended either to be despised or ignored.

133

The Chinese heritage

There were two kinds of Chinese culture. On the one hand there was the high culture, the 'great tradition' as it has been called, the literate, artistic, philosophic, history-conscious, pan-China culture of the élite. On the other there were the many sub-cultures, which belonged perhaps to small, not necessarily literate groups, bounded by dialects, which were the worlds within the Chinese world. The picture of Chinese society is of a large number of local culture cells all bound together by the high culture and its unifying activities and philosophies.

Throughout China's history dynasties have tried to bring her under strong central control. But even when the dynasties were set up by alien conquerors the cycle of dynastic growth and decline failed to shake the high Chinese culture. It needed the combination of a failing dynasty and the insistent expansionism of the mercantile west before China reluctantly began to concede that her cultural superiority was not absolute.

There had been contact with the west for many centuries. Christian missionaries gained a foothold at the Chinese court as early as 1601. But it was not until the early 19th century that western influence began seriously to be felt. China's self-sufficiency made her little interested in international trade. What little trade she had was in her favor as she had products such as tea, porcelain and silk to sell, which were much prized in the west. Only when a market in drugs was created and exploited by the British, with control of the Indian opium sources, did the trade balance swing the other way. Chinese government attempts to outlaw the opium trade and the opium habit proved fruitless. The coastal cell-like communities were quite deaf to the commands of the emperor in far Peking. The one serious attempt of a conscientious official (Lin Tse-hsu in 1839) to stop the trade led to the first Anglo-Chinese war and the first of the many humiliating defeats of China by western powers. Not only were western arms more effective, but China had never before been attacked from the south and east. By the end of the century the coastline was studded with enclaves of western influence. In some places land was leased; in others, such as Hong Kong, land was even ceded outright. The Ch'ing dynasty was fully dislodged in 1911 and a republic was set up. Democracy, science, capitalism, communism and other western concepts became a part of Chinese life.

But the mere existence of a republic was not sufficient to mend the shattered state, and the same localistic, cell-like fragmentation which had marked the declining decades of the dynasty remained. This situation developed until warlords ran huge areas of the country almost as separate states. A new kind of rural communism emerged and also began to carve out territory for itself. In 1937 Japan exploited this weakness and invaded China, capturing and holding until 1945 most of the key economic areas. After the Pacific War, by their dedication and superior organization, the communists were able to establish control over the entire country (except

134

About ten people were crushed or trampled to death in the rush to change paper money into gold in 1948 during the civil war.

A blind man led by a child on a leash holds up a basket for alms. The poorest people often sold their children to avoid starvation.

Workers pull a new lathe through Peking streets. Mao Tse-tung initiated an industrial as well as a communist revolution.

(Below) Defeated Nationalists flee the communists. Over 2 million accompanied Chiang Kai-shek to the offshore island of Taiwan.

An aging aristocrat, wrapped in her own indifference, walks along a Peking street through a world she can no longer recognize.

the large off-shore island of Taiwan), and localism once more lost ground to centralization.

With the advent of the republic in the early years of this century began a momentous reform, the 'plain speech' movement. This advocated bringing together the colloquial and the written word. The only effective way to do this was to seize upon one of the languages of China as a standard, and then to write everything in that one language. The use and teaching of Mandarin throughout China have since then been actively encouraged by successive governments, and the modern communication media have improved the possibilities for mass literacy in Mandarin. A limited number of simplifications and reforms of the characters themselves also contribute to the process.

In many ways the history of Chinese society has been a story of the tension between the cell and the whole. It is a tension which might be expressed as a conflict between centralization and decentralization. It remains an important feature of China today.

135

Glossary
to the peoples of the far east

China is the heartland of the mongoloid people. They are thought to have evolved there over a million years ago, and to have spread as far as the banks of the Volga, Madagascar and Tierra del Fuego. Physically they vary less than the Caucasoids or Africans for example. Their physical features are well known: skin pigmentation varies comparatively little in color; hair is black, grows long, rarely falls out and does not gray until very old age. Of medium height, they have long trunks with little lumbar curvature and relatively short arms and legs. Their eyes usually have an epicanthine or mongoloid fold under the lids. Their noses are either broad, flat and low-bridged, or aquiline.

Many of the peoples in this area, which includes China, Japan, Korea, Tibet, Nepal, Sikkim and Bhutan, have several different names, depending on who is referring to them. For example, the Ching-po are sometimes called the Kachin, the Jinghpaw or the Thienbaw. There is a list of alternative names at the end of the volume. The smaller groups of people tend to have fewer names. The commonest names of the major groups, as well as the Han, are the Ching-po, the Manchurians, the Mongols, the Nasi, the Pai, the Wa and the Yao.

HAN PEOPLES The Han peoples are the major group in China. They constitute 94 per cent of a Chinese population of nearly 800 million. They were relatively late arrivals in China and minorities distrusted them. Conversely, they regarded the non-Han peoples as aboriginal barbarians. They exercised power over the non-Han and collected taxes whenever they could, but never, until the Communists came to power, approached the non-Han strongholds.

NON-HAN MINORITIES More than 60 per cent of China's area is a virtually independent homeland for non-Han peoples, most of whom live in Sinkiang, Inner Mongolia, Tibet, the Muslim regions and the Chuang area of Kwangsi. The non-Han peoples of these areas range from tribal and semi-tribal societies to feudal and semi-feudal societies, with agricultural or mixed farming economies. They vary from almost naked cave-dwellers to people like the Nasi, who ruled a vast empire a thousand years ago. The Chinese government aims to preserve and protect their cultures and has encouraged the invention of scripts for unwritten languages and simplified the scripts of others. Where population or language information is not given about these groups in this glossary it is

because it has not yet been ascertained. There was no nationwide census of China until 1953. Before that population was reckoned by the number of families. In time there will be more details, but meanwhile there may well be some peoples whose very existence is unknown to us.

JAPANESE The Japanese are thought to have come into Japan from Korea sweeping the indigenous population who were probably Ainu (q.v.) northwards. They are, like the Chinese, mongoloid but their language remains something of a mystery. It has closer affinities to Polynesian, Turkish and Finnish languages than to the languages of mainland South-east Asia.

KOREANS For centuries Chinese cultural influences have seeped down from the north and a distinctive, fairly homogenous Korean national culture has developed. The Korean language is a branch of the Altaic group to which Turkish, Mongol and Tungus-Manchu belong, and seven dialects are spoken.

HIMALAYAN PEOPLES Many of the peoples in Bhutan, Sikkim and Nepal are mongoloids of Tibetan descent. There are also people of Indian descent, especially in Nepal in the western Himalayas.

ACHANG *Population:* 15,000. Language group: Tibeto-Burman. The Achang live scattered in Te-hung Thai and Ching-po Autonomous Chou in Yunnan province, south-west China. They are farmers and practise some handicrafts. They have no written script. Their religion is Hinayana Buddhism.

AINU (pages 38-43)

AKHA (pages 68-73)

BHOTE Bhote or Bhutia is a word used by Ghurkas to describe any of the Tibetan tribes settled within the borders of Nepal as well as Sikkimese (q.v.), Dukpa, Tamang (q.v.), and Sherpa (q.v.).

BHUTANESE (pages 82-87)

BHUTIA (see BHOTE)

CHEPANG *Population:* unknown. Language group: unknown. The Chepang are a nomadic forest tribe who live near the junction of the Kali, Seti and Trisuli rivers in east central Nepal. They are of Dravidian or of Turanian extraction, but speak their own language. They are few in number, and very shy. They used to live in caves and under trees; only recently have they been building temporary huts in the forest. They are a small people, dark and slight, with distinct Dravidian features that probably reflect their origin.

CHETRI *Population:* unknown. Language group: unknown. This powerful tribe, formerly called Kha, sprang from a mixture of two races: the offspring of Brahman refugees from the 12th century Muslim invasions of India, and local Nepalese hill women. The word Chetri is a corruption of the Sanskrit *kshatriya* and means 'a fighting man' or one of the warrior caste. The descendants of Rajput and other Kshatriya of the plains, who either sought refuge in Nepal or voluntarily served there as military advisors are known as Ektharia. They have since become completely fused with the Kha. In appearance the Chetri are generally slightly taller, slighter, darker and much hairier than the purely mongoloid tribes of Nepal. They are Hindus, intermarry only among themselves and enjoy a high social standing in Nepal. Their customs resemble the practices of orthodox Hinduism and they are dominated by Brahman guidance.

CH'IANG *Population:* 30,000. Language group: Tibeto-Burman. The Ch'iang live in A-pa Tibetan Autonomous Chou, Mao-wen Ch'iang Autonomous County and Sung-p'an and Li counties in Szechwan Province. They are farmers and craftsmen. Their language is still unwritten. Their religion is pantheistic.

CH'I-LAO *Population:* 20,500. Language group: Kadai. The Ch'i-lao (also known as I-lao, Kei-lao, Kelao, Kha Lao, Khi Lao, Thi, Thu and Xan Lao) live in Kuan-ling, Lang-tai, Ch'ien-hsi and Chih-chin counties, and in Kweichow, Lung-lin Multinational Autonomous County in Kwangsi Chuang Autonomous region. They are farmers, do handicrafts and have a pantheistic religion.

CHING-PO *Population:* 100,000 in China. Language group: Tibeto-Burman. The Ching-po tribes (also known as Chingpaw, Jinghpaw, Kachin, Kakhieng, Singhpo and Thienbaw) live in Te-hung Thai and Ching-po Autonomous Chou in Yunnan Province. Outside China they live in Tibet and Burma. They live mainly in the hills, where they cultivate rice by the slash-and-burn method. The Ching-po were never Buddhists. Their society traditionally included two main forms of political organization: *gumlao* and *gumsa*. *Gumlao* was democratic, with the village as the political unit and no class distinctions. *Gumsa* was aristocratic and the political unit was the territory known as *mung*, headed by an aristocratic prince. Free movement across the China-Burma border was essential for the Burmese Ching-po, who depended on their Chinese counterparts for all goods and tools such as plow-blades, hoes, swords, pots and pans. Their rituals, such as ancestor worship, also came from China. Ching-po have been influenced by their neighbors, especially the Shan.

CH'IU-TZU *Population:* unknown. Language group: unknown. The Ch'iu-tzu, who live north of the Mekong-Salween divide in the province of Chinghai, call themselves Trun and are related to the Lu-tzu (q.v.) of the Salween. They live beyond the great snow range of the Mekong, and belong to the wild tribes of the western region of Ho-ch'ing and Li-chiang. Their dwellings are made of braided grass, covered with the bark of trees. Men wear short hemp-cloth garments and no shoes, with their hair long and disheveled. Women wear similar clothes and large copper earrings. They grow various kinds of millet. They are not war-like, fear the Lu-tzu and dare not enter their territory alone or uninvited. Many hire themselves to the Lu-tzu as farm laborers. They protect their feet from thorns and insect bites by putting resin from pine trees on the soles, rubbing them with dust and repeating this several times. The Lolo (q.v.) also have this custom. Little is known of their political organization, religious beliefs or marriage customs. They are a very peaceful and friendly people.

CHUANG *Population:* 6,611,455 in China. Language: Northern Tai. The Chuang live in Kwangsi Chuang Autonomous Region, Wen-shan Chuang and Miao Autonomous Chou of Yunnan Province, Tung-hsiang Multinational Autonomous County of Kwangtung, Lien-shan Chuang and Yao Autonomous County of Kwangtung, and in Kweichow in southern China. The Chuang are farmers and their religious beliefs are pantheistic.

DAGHOR *Population:* 44,100. Language: Altaic. The Daghor (also known as Dagur, Daur, Ta-kuan-erb, Ta-hu-erh) live in Tsi-Tsi-har Municipality and Fu-yu County in Heilungkiang, and scattered in Mo-li-ta-wa Daghor Autonomous Banner, Pu-t'e-ha Banner, O-wen-k'o Autonomous Banner in Inner Mongolia, T'a-ch'eng County in Sinkiang Uighur Autonomous Region, northern China. They are farmers and lamaist Buddhists who have not forgotten their ancient pantheistic beliefs and practices.

ETA *Population:* over 2 million. Language: Japanese. Though not racially distinct from other Japanese, the Eta are outcasts whose presence is considered to be polluting. They live in widely scattered communities throughout Japan and still work in leather industries, in slaughter-houses, and in graveyards and crematoria – these being the occupations which earned them their outcaste status centuries ago. It was under the influence of Buddhism from China that, by the 10th century AD, contact with death or blood came to be considered polluting. Many Japanese would still feel defiled if their house were visited by an Eta, and would throw salt around to purify it. There is strong prejudice against marriage with Eta. Their difficult position in modern society has been neglected by governments, and they are now organized in political associations to make their voice heard. The total number of Eta is difficult to assess.

GHARTI *Population:* unknown. Language group: unknown. The Gharti, one of the six Magar (q.v.) tribes, live in western Nepal. They do not speak the Magar language and differ in physical appearance from the three main Magar tribes. Their exact origin is obscure. It seems highly likely they were all freed slaves; until recently slaves were invariably called Gharti. The Gharti of today refuse to admit that such a stigma attaches to their name. The Gharti are chiefly shepherds.

GURKHAS The Gurkhas of Nepal are world famous as soldiers. They are not a tribe in themselves but consist of Gurung (q.v.), Limbu (q.v.), Magar (q.v.) and Rai (q.v.) peoples.

GURUNG *Population:* unknown. Language group: Tibeto-Burman. The Gurung proper are of Mongolian descent, but their precise origin remains unknown. They live in the highlands in the eastern and northern parts of central Nepal, and lead a pastoral, agricultural way of life. Gurung are divided into two distinct classes: char-jat and solah-jat Gurung. Today these once great social distinctions are largely disappearing and intermarriage between the classes is fairly widespread. Gurung divide time into cycles of twelve years known as Barkha. Each of these cycles is given the name of an animal. Every child is carefully taught the Barkha in which his birth took place. After the birth of each child the mother is considered unclean for eleven days. During this time she is segregated from all contact with outsiders, and especially from any men of her own household. On the

137

eleventh day a priest, either a lama or a Brahman, performs the naming ceremony for the child. This is the occasion for a big feast of cooked rice, meat, fowl and home-brewed beer. At the end of the ceremony the mother is considered to be pure again and is free to leave her house at will. Marriage dates are usually set after consulting astrologers. A Gurung is usually buried in a place set aside for the purpose just outside the village. Very close relatives will mourn for 13 days, during which period they may eat only rice and only once a day. A single layer of white clothes may be worn. A funeral ceremony, *aghun*, which is like an Irish wake, is attended by other mourners; large quantities of food and liquor are consumed. Gurung dress much like other inhabitants of central Nepal. One sartorial peculiarity is the *rup*, a yellow cord worn around the neck. Men wear it with nine, and women seven, strands and knots. It is meant to ward off evil spirits and misfortune, and is placed around the neck by the wearer's mother.

HA-NI *Population:* 480,000 in China. Language group: Tibeto-Burman. The Ha-ni (also known as Houni and Woni) live in Hung-ho Ha-ni and I Autonomous Chou and Chaing-ch'eng Ha-ni and I Autonomous County in Yunnan Province. They are also scattered in Hsi-shuang Pan-na Thai Autonomous Chou in Yunnan, south-west China. They are farmers and their religious beliefs are pantheistic. A new script is being introduced to supplement their hitherto oral language.

HLI-KHIN *Population:* unknown. Language group: unknown. The Hli-khin live in the north-east of Yunnan Province and are the main inhabitants of Yung-ning. They mainly belong to the Yellow Lama Church (Gelug-ba sect), but their original shamanistic religion still exists and is practised by the few remaining sorcerers *(nda-pa)*.
Their rituals are performed out of doors, in a meadow, and are reputed to end in general drunkenness. Since they have no written language *nda-pa* must chant all ceremonies from memory. Hli-khin have unusual marriage customs. The girl remains at home and takes a husband whom she keeps for as long as she likes, and then may send him away and take another. Her brother is responsible for her and her children's welfare. Venereal diseases were reportedly common among the Hli-khin before the Revolution. Suicide among them is unknown.

HSI-FAN *Population:* 15,000. Languages: Tibetan and Chinese. The Hsi-fan live in the north-west mountains of Yunnan province. They once occupied the entire Li-chiang territory but were conquered by the Mo-so-man (Nasi q.v.) during the T'ang dynasty and were driven north. In an attempt to recapture Li-chiang in about 1521 they were defeated and most were decapitated at a place known as Boa-shi, 'dead Boa'. (Hsi-fan are also known as Boa and P'u). They have no written language, but lamas have used Tibetan to record it. Most Hsi-fan were converted to the church of the Yellow Lama when a Buddha came to live among them about 400 years ago. But some adhered to the shamanistic sect of the Black Bon Lama and still practise its magic. The sect of shamanists, called Ha-pa practised blood sacrifices. The Hsi-fan cremate their dead and deposit the ashes on the limestone cliffs of Mount Hla-dze, which they regard as the cradle of their race. Both men and women wear skirts – the men's striped horizontally, the women's longitudinally.

KAZAKH *Population:* 500,000 in China. Language group: Altaic (Turkic) with Roman alphabet. The Kazakh, who also live in Kazakhastan, live in I-li Kazakh Autonomous Chou, in Sinkiang Uighur Autonomous Region and in Kansu and Singhai Provinces in north-west China. They are farmers and keep animals. Many of them are still nomadic, and follow Islam.

KIRANTI *Population:* unknown. Language group: Tibeto-Burman. Kiranti is the collective name for the tribes of eastern Nepal who have become so intermixed and have so many similar customs that it is convenient to group them together. Large numbers live in Sikkim. They include the Limbu (q.v.) and the Rai (q.v., also known as Khambu or Yakka). Intermarriage is common among the members of the tribes, although the women remain members of the tribe into which they were born.

KIRGHIZ *Population:* 70,000 in China. Language group: Altaic (Turkic). The Kirghiz, who also live in Turkey and Russia, live in K'o-tzu-lo-su Kirghiz Autonomous Chou in Sinkiang Uighur Autonomous

Region. They are Muslims who farm and breed animals.

KOREANS (pages 62-67)

LAHU (pages 68-73)

LEPCHA *Population:* unknown. Language group: unknown. The Lepcha come from

138

Sikkim, but a number of them have lived in Nepal for many generations. They live in Ilam and Dhankuta and many have emigrated to the Darjeeling and Kalimpong area. The Lepcha are primarily animists, but they have been affected by Lamaist Buddhism, and in Darjeeling many are Christians. A superstitious people, the Lepcha spend much of their time appeasing evil spirits and are reputed to practise witchcraft and cast spells. They know the jungle well, especially the herbs and poisons. Some of them live off the land, others are employed as house-servants or clerks in the towns.

LHARDEI *Population*: unknown. Language group: unknown. The Lhardei live in a mountain valley on the Chinghai-Szechwan border, north-west of Dzorgei. They live in four villages of polygonal, black yak wool tents, which they move to opposite sides of the valley depending on the season. They pay tribute of cattle, butter and milk to the lamas of Lhabrang who are the real rulers of the Lhardei. But their temporal interests are entrusted by the lamas to the superior of the lamasery which stands on the mountainside. There is no wood at all in this valley and for fuel Lhardei are completely dependent on *argol*, dried-out animal droppings. They keep *pinyu* which are yak crossed with domestic cows. When the Lhardei are on the move they do not put up tents at night but simply undo the belts holding up their sheepskins so that they drop over their feet. Then they turn their collars up over their ears, turn the woolly borders of their caps down and thus cocooned they lie down in the snow allowing it to cover them like a warm blanket.

LI *Population*: 360,000 in China. Language: Kadai. The Li (also known as B'lai, B'li, Dai Dli, Hiai, K'lai, Lai, Le, Loi and S'lai) live in Li and Miao Autonomous Chou on Hainan Island of Kwangtung Province, Kwangsi Chuang Autonomous Region, Yunnan and Hunan Provinces in southern China. They are farmers, and have a newly invented script. Their religious beliefs are pantheistic, although some are Taoists.

LIMBU *Population*: unknown. Language group: unknown. The Limbu live in the country between the Tamba Kosi and the Mechi, in eastern Nepal, where they are the oldest recorded population. Their flat features, slightly oblique yellow eyes, beardlessness and yellow complexions suggest that they may be the descendants of early Tibetan settlers in Nepal. A Limbu may marry any girl he likes, provided she does not belong to his tribe. A common way of choosing and courting a bride is by open singing contests held for this very purpose. The man or the girl begins by singing a couplet, to which the other must reply. The couplets are made up on the spur of the moment, and each one must be wittier or funnier than the one before it. The competition goes on until the man can make the girl tongue-tied, and then he has won her. If he fails to do so, he must give way to other suitors. The Limbu, unlike the peoples of western and central Nepal, usually contract marriage without parental consent, at a relatively late age. It is common among poorer people for the parents of the bride to know nothing at all of their daughter's marriage until she returns from the ceremony. The Limbu bury their dead.

LISU *Population*: 300,000. Language group: Tibeto-Burman. The Lisu live in the Salween river valley, south of Lyu-ra-gang, and about 18 miles south of Yung-ning in Yunnan Province. They keep sheep and yaks and grow maize, which, with millet and pumpkins, is their staple food. Lisu houses are regularly shaped yellow pine log cabins, with roofs made of pine boards weighted down with rocks or, in the pumpkin season, with all the pumpkin crop. Lisu women wear plaited wigs of black cotton thread, with red dyed yak or horse hair tied to the ends. They also wind around their heads strings of thick discs of white conch shells, interspersed with a reddish transparent cornelian. They wear short pleated, hemp cloth skirts which they weave themselves from the fiber of the female *cannabis sativa* plant. The children go naked.

LOLO *Population*: over 3 million. Language group: Tibeto-Burman. The Lolo (also known as Hei-i, T'ou, I, I-chia, Leisu, Lo-kuei, Man-chia, Man-tzu, Mosu, Neisu, Nesu, Ngosu, No, Norsu, Nosu, Pei-i, Ku-t'ou – all collectively known as Yi) live in and around the mountains of Liang Shan which is the common frontier of Szechwan, Sinkiang and Yunnan Provinces. One of the largest minority groups in China, the Lolo live in a feudal system with princes of Chinese ancestry at the top of the hierarchy. These aristocrats are of true Lolo blood and are called the Black Lolo, serfs of freed descendants of slaves of foreign origin. Beneath the White Lolo come people who are called neither Black nor White, a group of slaves who are fairly well treated but not free. These different classes are of different stock, and have different activities. The White Lolo and slaves do farm work, cultivating oats, barley, buckwheat and potatoes. The Black Lolo are herdsmen and practise all the skills of war. Every lord has a suit of leather armor, and a lance almost 30 feet long, and is served by a squire. The Black Lolo must never intermarry with any other class and they are so jealous of the purity of their blood that if illicit relations between one of their women and a White Lolo are discovered, the two offenders are expected to commit suicide or are put to death. Thus the Lolo effectively have a caste system. Rival Black Lolo clans are constantly feuding, backed compulsorily by their serfs and slaves. Their houses are wooden and surrounded by bamboo stockades. Dogs are crucified and left as signs on land that is claimed by two or more clans. The Black Lolo have scribes who record important events in family history, and who divine which spirits are responsible for illnesses, and cure them with appropriate spells. The White Lolo, descendants of slaves, have adopted Lolo ways and are accepted by the Black Lolo into their own culture. There are about ten White Lolo families to each Black Lolo household. Being a class of serfs the White Lolo have rights in houses, property and land in return for certain economic obligations owed to their Black lords. In feuds between Black clans, the White serfs must fight for their masters, and the Black lord must, for his part, take care of his serfs or they will offer allegiance to another.

LU-TZU *Population*: 13,000. Language group: Tibeto-Burman. The Lu-tzu (also called Nu-tzu, Nu and A-nu) live in the Salween river valley from Lyu-ra-gang in the south to Sang-tha in the north. North of them are Tibetans, and to the south are the Black Lisu (q.v.). They live entirely isolated from the rest of the world for five months of every year when their valley is snowed up. They are a calm, amiable people who are great hunters. Every child carries a cross-bow and shoots every bird in sight, while the men hunt tigers and leopards. They practise slash-and-burn agriculture and their staple foods are wheat, millet and coarse vegetables, yam and taro. Though the Lu-tzu live in a wooded area, the roofs of their houses are made of bamboo and the walls of braided bamboo. They make bamboo utensils and weave red designs into their hemp cloth. Their garments are of hemp cloth. The men wear trousers, the women skirts, and all go barefoot. Men and women have their faces tattooed from the age of ten with flowers, dragons and phoenixes.

MAGAR *Population:* unknown. Language group: Tibeto-Burman. The Magar live mostly in that part of central Nepal which is to the south of the Gurung (q.v.) country and extends north to the flanks of the Himalayan range. There are Magar colonies all over Nepal where they represent nearly a third of the total population. Because of their geographical position, the Magar were among the first of the Nepalese tribes to receive immigrants from the plains of India. As a result their customs, and particularly their religion, are more closely related to orthodox Hinduism than those of other tribes. Brahman have some priestly duties. Others are still undertaken by their own *jhankris*. Many Magar are shepherds. Because of the difficulty of producing rice in the high country, the staple diet of those who farm is barley.

MANCHURIAN *Population:* 2,419,000 in China. Language group: Altaic. The Manchurians (also known as Man and Manchu) live in Liaoning, Heilungkiang, Kirin and Hopeh Provinces, Peking city, Inner Mongolian Autonomous region; they are also scattered in Shantung, Hupeh, Szechwan, Kansu, Hunan, Kwangtung and other provinces. The formation of the Manchu power that invaded China in the 17th century began when a number of small tribes akin in race and speech, but widely scattered, joined forces. They possessed no sense of political or tribal unity, ranging from settled people in walled towns – the Old Manchu – to the inhabitants of forest clearings who were part hunters and part farmers and to reindeer nomads and hunting groups – the New Manchu. Today the Manchurians' socio-economic organization is still very varied although many have clearly been affected by Chinese influence over the centuries. The Manchu Ch'ing dynasty replaced the Chinese house of Ming in the Imperial capital of Peking in 1644. Ch'ing emperors learned to speak and write Chinese and their own language fell into disuse. Although certain government posts were reserved for Manchu, most civil servants were Chinese. The military organization of the Manchu, however, combined with the resources of China was

powerful enough to add Mongolia, Sinkiang and Tibet to the Manchu-Chinese empire, doubling the extent of China.

MIAO-TZE *Population:* over 2·5 million. Language group: Miao-yao. The Miao-tze live on the joint Kweichow and Kwangsi border area (in south Kweichow and north Kwangsi) and in Hunan, Yunnan, Szechwan, Chekiang, Kwangtung, Fukien and Hupeh Provinces and Kwangsi Chuang Autonomous Region. According to Miao-tze tradition the country they now live in was once inhabited by other people: the Yao (q.v.) and the Kelilao. The Miao-tze originated from Hunan or Kwangsi, took the area by force and massacred its people. They were in turn conquered by the Tai, who followed them from the same regions of central China. From then onwards the two peoples occupied the same territories but in separate villages and obeying different chiefs. Most village chiefdoms of the Miao-tze were not hereditary, but appointed, or at least approved, by the Chinese authorities during the Empire. At times of revolt the Miao-tze have remained aloof while the Tai were active. The submission of the Miao-tze to imperial authority was caused both by their lack of tribal cohesion and unity and by their former defeat by the Tai. The Miao-tze are distinguished by their great love of dancing. At marriages, feasts and funerals they relate the events of the Creation and the Deluge according to their own oral tradition which bears an extraordinary resemblance to similar

accounts in the Bible. Until recently they had no script. The women wear knee-length skirts, and a low-cut bodice with a sailor collar.

MONGOLS *Population:* over 1·5 million. Language group: Altaic. The Mongols live in the Inner Mongolian Autonomous Region, Liaoning, Sinkiang Uighur Autonomous Region, Kirin, Heilungkiang, Tsinghai, Hopeh, Honan, Szechwan, Kansu, Hunan, Kwangtung and other provinces. Originally a nomadic pastoral people, the Mongols (also known as Mongolians and Meng) had an economy entirely based on their flocks and herds. These provided every necessity of housing, clothing and food – largely meat and dairy produce. Everything which could be bought or sold for money was therefore pure luxury. If a Mongol could sell the surplus of his herd to obtain cloth, grain and manufactured articles, his standard of living was higher than that of the Chinese peasant. As they enjoy leisure, which they associate with dignity, the Mongols tend to avoid doing unnecessary work. They prefer to go hunting or to ride away to visit friends. The pastoral Mongol lives in a felt tent which is cool in hot weather, but warm in the cold. He uses cattle dung as fuel for his fire. With his milk and meat he eats far better than peasants who turn good pasture into poor arable land and toil in the rice fields. But the population growth and immigration into traditional Mongol territories by others are forcing the Mongols either to give up their herds or to go elsewhere.

MUSLIMS *Population:* 10 million. Language: Chinese. Islam was introduced in China by traders in the 7th century AD. The Chinese Muslims (also known as Ho, Hui, Hui-tze, Hwei, Pang-hse, Panthay, Panthe, and Panthee) live mainly in Ning-hsia Hui Autonomous Chou of Kansu, Honan, Hopeh, Tsinghai, Shantung and Yunnan and other provinces. The Muslims have always acted as a nation within China. They are mainly farmers, but some are merchants.

NASI *Population:* 140,000. Language group: Tibeto-Burman. The Nasi live in Li-chiang Autonomous County and scattered in Wei-shi Chung-tien, Ning-slang and Yung-sheng Counties in Yunnan, south-west China. Most Nasi are farmers and keep animals. A few are tradesmen and others specialize in handicrafts. The most primitive type of Nasi live undisturbed where they first settled there many years ago, in the districts of Ha-ba and Bber-dder in the south-eastern part of the Chungtien triangle. Here they follow their old religious customs – a mixture of pantheistic shamanism and the pre-Buddhist Bon religion of Tibet and there are no lamas or lama temples or lamaseries as in the Li-chiang district, nor are there any Chinese temples. Nasi territory is difficult to reach, and this has kept them isolated and largely unchanged. They have come into little contact with the Chinese, but have been exposed in the north to Tibetan (q.v.) bandit invasion when they fled unarmed to the hills. The Nasi cremate their dead. Their sorcerers exorcize the demons of disease. In the remote areas of Chung-tien they practise the ancient ceremony of *muan-bpo* (propitiation of Heaven). The Nasi are a scrupulously polite people. The men are tall and well-built. They wear home-spun hemp cloth trousers, jackets of colors ranging from white to light gray, and wear straw sandals or go barefoot. The front half of their heads is shaven, the hair at the back is plaited. They say the Tibetans, whom they still fear, would kill them if they dispensed with this plait.

NEWAR *Population:* unknown. Language group: Tibeto-Burman. The Newar were the main inhabitants of the Katmandu Valley in the 14th century – as they are today – but their origins are unknown. Their language and customs suggest that they originated north of the Himalayas. Their original culture was profoundly influenced by Buddhists and later by Hindu refugees fleeing the Muslim invasion of India. They are the skilled craftsmen of Nepal – in metal work, sculpture, painting, architecture and literature. Where they live outside the Katmandu Valley they tend to work as shop-keepers. Five to twelve years old Newar girls are married to Narain, the god of the harvest and of fertility, who has the shape of a *bel* fruit. Each girl is given a *bel* fruit with a few inches of stalk attached at a ceremony performed by a priest. As the wife of the immortal Narain a Newar woman is theoretically free to leave her earthly husband; adultery is treated lightly; and she is not considered a widow when her earthly husband dies.

NUNG *Population:* 190,000 in China. Language group: Tai. The Nung live scattered in south-east Yunnan, south-west China. They are farmers and their religious beliefs are pantheistic.

PAI *Population:* 560,000 in China. Language group: Tibeto-Burman. The Pai live in Ta-li Pai Autonomous Chou in Yunnan and other parts of Yunnan Province in south-west China. The Pai (also known as Ber Dser, Ber Wa Dser, La Bhu, Min-chia, Min-chia-tzu, Pai-jen, Pai-man, Per-nu-tuu, Per-tsu, Pe-tsen, Pe-tso, Petsu Shua Ber Ni) are said to be the original and principal population of the ancient Nan-chao kingdom. Around Tai-li they have extensively intermingled with other tribes. They extend north from there to Ho-ch'ing and thence south-west: where they occupy the valley of the P'i Chiang with its two towns, Yunlung and Lan-p'ing exclusively. Most of the Pai are farmers, but some work in industry and commerce. Pai women are recognizable by their brilliant red trousers. Some Pai women carry heavy loads by means of a yoke secured by a head strap. The Pai custom of covering their two front teeth with gold earned them the name 'Chin-ch'ih-man', which means 'gold-teeth savages'. The Pai have no written language. Their religion is pantheistic, with much sorcery. Some have become Buddhists or Christians.

PAN-YU *Population:* unknown. Language group: unknown. The Pan-yu (or Pain-yu) live in the mountains of the Szechwan-Chingai-Kansu border. They are the first tribe of the Dzorgei confederation of 12 tribes. They herd yak, goats and sheep. Their chiefs' authority is limited. All heads of families participate in important decisions of change of residence, and war and peace. Otherwise each tribe and indeed each family acts independently, raiding and pillaging as they choose. Although their social ties are lax, relations between the tribes tend to be good. All tribes would come to the aid of any member if attacked. In their Arctic climate they wear nothing but a hooded mantle of sheepskin edged with a collar of panther skin, which they often hitch up or drop off their shoulders leaving large parts of their bodies exposed to the cold. They also wear boots and on long journeys, a conical sheepskin hat over their cropped hair which can be rolled over the ears. They are fine horsemen and carry swords, muskets or rifles, and enormous lances. They live with their animals and protected by ferocious dogs in subterranean dwellings which look from the outside like natural hillocks. Inside they are hollows of 30 to 50 feet in diameter and 10 to 12 feet high, with thick beams and pillars supporting the earth. They eat the meat of yak, goat and sheep and their milk and cream. They drink hot buttered tea.

PULANG *Population:* 35,000 in China. Language group: Mon-Khmer. The Pulang (also known as Humai, Palaung and Rumai) live scattered in Hsi-shuang Pan-na Thai Autonomous Chou and Lan-ts'ang Lak-ku Autonomous County in Yunnan Province south-west China. They are Buddhists and farmers.

PUYI *Population:* 1,248,000. Language group: Tai. The Puyi (also known as Chung-chia, Dioi, I-chia, I-jen, Jao-chia, Jui, Pu-i, Pu-yueh, Shui-hu, Pen-ti and Yoi) live in Pu-i and Miao Autonomous Chou in Kweichow, and in other counties in Kweichow, Yunnan and Szechwan Provinces, south-west China. They are farmers and their religion is pantheistic.

RAI *Population:* unknown. Language group: unknown. The Rai have much in common with, and have intermarried with, the Limbu (q.v.). The Rai believe they are surrounded by a multitude of nameless and capricious evil spirits who are appeased and propitiated by Biuwas, a class of wandering mendicants peculiar to Sikkim and eastern Nepal. Today the Rai unenthusiastically recognize Brahman and employ them to cast horoscopes and choose children's names and dates for marriages. The Rai's special god is their ancestral household deity Parabhang who they worship in March and November with the sacrifice of a pig and offerings of incense and *murwa* beer. They honor Parabhang more highly than the Hindu divinity Devi, to whom they occasionally sacrifice buffalo, goats, fowl and pigeons. Rai girls marry – today without a bride-price – when they are adults. Sexual license is tolerated before marriage on the rarely broken understanding that a man marries a girl he makes pregnant. Divorce, granted on grounds of adultery, is rare. The Rai bury their dead with a few personal possessions.

RUSSIANS *Population:* 20,000 in China. 141

Language group: Indo-European. The Russians live in I-ning and Urumchi Municipalities, and T'a-ch'eng County in Sinkiang Uighur Autonomous Region. Most of them are farmers, though some are businessmen living in towns. Their religion is Russian-Orthodox.

SA-LA *Population:* 30,600. Language group: Altaic (Turkic). The Sa-la (also known as Salar) live in Hsun-hus Salar county of Tsing-hai, Hua-ling Hui Autonomous County of Tsing-hai, Lin-hsia County, Hsi-ning and Lin-t'an districts of Kansu, northern China. They are mainly farmers but some are merchants. Most are Muslims.

SHE *Population:* 210,000. Language: Miao-yao. The She (also called Sho) live in Fu-an Special District in Fukien, Wen-chow and Chin-hua special districts in Che-kiang. They are also scattered in Ch'ien-shan and Kwei-chi in Kiangsi Province, and in Ch'ao-an in Kwangtung Province, south-east China. They are farmers of pantheistic beliefs, and speak mostly Chinese, although they still have their own language.

SHERPA *Population:* unknown. Language group: Tibetan. The Sherpa live throughout the uplands of eastern Nepal, and many of them have settled in Darjeeling. But their true home is in the Solo Khumbu area in the upper reaches of the Dudh Kosi. Because of the altitude, they can only grow barley, maize and potatoes, and selling seed potatoes is one of their main sources of income. The Sherpa are more closely related to the Tibetans than to the other tribes of eastern Nepal. They are Buddhists of the Lama of the Red Hat sect who are allowed to marry. They are extremely strong and are able to carry very heavy loads for long distances at high altitudes. The Sherpa are world-famous as porters for Himalayan mountaineering expeditions. Tenzing Norkay shared with the British mountaineer Sir Edmund Hillary the distinction of being the first to reach the summit of Mount Everest in 1953.

SHUI *Population:* 130,000. Language group: Kam-Sui-Mak. The Shui (also known as Shui-chia and Sui) live in San-tu Shui

Autonomous County in Kweichow Province, and Kwangsi Chuang Autonomous Region. They are farmers with a pantheistic religion.

SIBO *Population:* 10,000. Language group: Altaic. The Sibo (also called Hsi-po) live in Ch'a-pu-ch'a-erh Sibo Autonomous County in Sinkiang Uighur Autonomous Region, and are also scattered in Kirin and Liaoning Provinces, north-east China. They are farmers whose religious beliefs center on shamanism.

SUNWAR *Population:* unknown. Language group: unknown. The Sunwar are a small agricultural tribe who live in eastern Nepal. Their customs conform closely to those of the Magar (q.v.) and like them they employ Brahman only in certain of their religious ceremonies, to read horoscopes, and choose names for children and marriage dates. They marry from the age of five and may not marry their cousins. On the death of a close relation, the Sunwar shave their eyebrows, head and moustache and may wear only one layer of white clothing and no hat. Mourning lasts for ten days for a parent, wife or married brother, but only five days for unmarried brothers and sisters. Married women are mourned only by their husband's family, never by their own.

TAI *Population:* 470,000. Language group: Tai. The Tai (or Dioi) live in country extending from Kweichow and Kwangsi through Yunnan and over the border into North Vietnam, north Laos and Thailand. They are a peasant people who grow rice on terraces. Their houses are built on the hillsides. Above a cellar used as a stable stairs lead to a large room, in which the ancestors are supposed to live, with several small rooms on either side. All Tai are closely united. A man of any Tai village is received and looked after everywhere with great hospitality, and in times of war all Tai are quick to help their fellow countrymen.

TAIWAN ABORIGINES (see pages 44-49)

TAJIK *Population:* 14,000 in China. Language group: Indo-European. The Tajik are nomadic herdsmen of central Asia. Some

live in Tashurgan Tadshik Autonomous County, P'i-shan, Yen-ch'eng and Sha-ch'e Counties in Sinkiang Uighur Autonomous Region. They are Muslim.

TAMANG *Population:* unknown. Language group: unknown. The Tamang (also known as Murmi) probably entered Nepal through the valleys of the Buri Gandak and Trisuli rivers, and settled north-west of Katmandu. From there they pushed on east. Today they live in large villages in that area, and in the northern parts of Ghorka and the eastern parts of Lamjung. There they live side by side with the Ghale. Their physical appearance and the fact that their clans have Tibetan names suggests that they may be of Tibetan descent. They are similar in language and customs in many respects to the Gurung (q.v.). They practise an animistic, lamaistic Buddhism. A Tamang village is easily recognized by its display of prayer flags and by *mane* walls along the roadside. They generally cremate their dead, but often bury young children who die.

TATZE *Population:* unknown. Language group: unknown. The Tatze live in the mountains of the Chinghai-Kansu-Szechwan border areas, and particularly in the valley of Seirachong. They are a pastoral nomadic people, who recognize no chiefs but follow leaders who show skill. They live in round white felt tents fixed to an umbrella-like wooden framework with wooden doors as well as flaps resembling the Mongol *yurt*. The tents can be easily packed, moved, expanded and contracted. Except for short stops, they build earthern fires in the middle of the floor which divide the tent into two. The left part is reserved for men and the right part for women. Their furniture – an altar to the ancestors, small chests and side-boards – is rare among nomads. They have their heads completely shaven except for a small lock of hair, and wear a long sheepskin coat, furry boots and a cap with a tassel. Recently they have added short trousers to the outfit.

THAKALI *Population:* unknown. Language: Thakalikura. The Thakali live in Nepal in the steep valley of the Upper Kali between Dana and Mukinath, the territory of the Punyel to whom they are distantly related and are similar. They are said to originate from the village of Thak, and to have taken their name from it. Thakali women run many of the inns (*bhattis*) along the main routes of central Nepal. The Thakali are mostly borax and salt traders, and they use sheep which they breed themselves as beasts of burden, and resemble the Tibetans. Their religion is lamaistic.

THAKURI *Population:* unknown. Language: unknown. The Thakuri, a Gurkha people (q.v.), have the highest social standing, apart from Brahman, of all Gurkhas. Of the Thakuri the Shah, of which the King of Nepal is himself a member, is the clan with the highest status. All Thakuri claim to be equal, except those who have the royal status of the Shahs. Their social organization is simple compared with that of most other Gurkha tribes and only a few clans divide into lineages. Thakuri caste beliefs are limited.

THARU *Population:* unknown. Language: unknown. The Tharu live in Terai, which extends practically all the way along the southern boundary of Nepal. In this malarial area only the Tharu can remain all the year. They are thought to be its aboriginal inhabitants. They live in small hamlets in the middle of isolated cultivated patches. They are chiefly employed as *dak*, runners and elephant riders. In the hot, rainy season they are employed catching wild elephants – a difficult and dangerous job.

TIBETANS (pages 74-81)

T'U *Population:* 53,000. Language: Altaic. The T'u (or Monguor) live in Hu-chu Tu Autonomous County in Tsinghai and scattered in Min-ho and Ta-t'ung Counties in Tsinghai and in Kansu Province as well as on the banks of the Kwang Ho above Lan-chou in north central China. They speak Chinese in everyday life and Tibetan in religious ceremonies, but retain their own language. They are farmers and their religion is lamaism.

T'UCHIA *Population:* 300,000. Language: Tibeto-Burman. They live in T'u-chia and Miao Autonomous Chou in Hunan, Lai-feng, Ho-feng and Yien Counties in Hupeh province, south-east China. They are farmers and practise some handicrafts. They are Muslim.

TUNG *Population:* 700,000. Language: Kam-Sui-Mak, possibly related to Tai. The Tung (also called Kam, Nin Kam, Tung-chia and Tung-jen) live in Miao and Tung Autonomous Chou in Kweichow, San-chiang T'ung Autonomous County in Kwangsi Chuang Autonomous Region, Hsin-huang T'ung and T'ung-tao T'ung Autonomous Counties in Hunan. They are farmers and woodsmen. Their religious beliefs are pantheistic.

TUNG-HSIANG *Population:* 150,000. Language: Altaic. The Tung-shiang live in Tung-hsiang Autonomous County in Kansu and scattered in Kuang-ho, Ho-cheng and Lin-hsia Counties in Kansu, north China. They have no script and are Muslim.

UIGHUR *Population:* over 3 million in China. Language: Altaic. The Uighur (also known as Hui-hu, Kao-ch'e, Uygur, Ughuri, Wei-ur and Wei-wu-erh) live in Kashgaria and the I-li regions of Dzungaria in Sinkiang Uighur Autonomous Region. A few have settled in T'ao yuan County of Hunan. They are farmers, rear animals and practise handicrafts. They are Muslim.

UZBEK *Population:* 13,000 in China. Language: Altai. The Uzbek (also known as Wu'tzu-pieh-k'o) are a Muslim central Asian people who also live in small numbers in

I-ning and Urunchi cities and T'a-Ch'eng and Sha-ch'e Counties of Sinkiang Uighur Autonomous Region and in Tung-peh. Most live in towns and work in business or handicrafts. A few are farmers.

WA *Population:* 280,000. Language group: Mon-Khmer. The Wa (also known as Kawa, Hai, Hkawa, Hkun, K'a-la, La, Lai-wa, Lawa, Loi-la, Nyo, Tai Loi, Vu and Wa Wu) live in Meng-lien Thai, La-ku and K'a-wa Autonomous County, Lan-t'sang, La-ku Autonomous County, Ts'ang-yuan K'a-wa Autonomous County, and Hsi-meng K'a-wa Autonomous County in Yunnan Province, south-west China. Their staple food is rice to which they add meat from hunting. They used to produce cash-crops of poppies for opium, and much of their land was so poor that they could not have survived without this source of income. The Wa also used to be called the Wild Wa, and were famous as head hunters— probably for political as well as religious motives. They had a marked preference for Chinese heads. They may have played a role in the complex political and economic system in which the northern Shan states subsisted on trade with Chinese caravaners by regulating the flow of trade. The Wa head-hunters and their chiefs seem to have been, among other things, bandits and toll-collectors along the caravan routes. They may also have been pawns in the incessant rivalries between Shan princes.

YAO *Population:* 660,000 in China. Language group: Miao-Yao. The Yao (also called Iu Mien, Kim Mien, Kim Mun, Lingnan,

Yao-man and Yu-Mien) and live in Laos, Thailand, and North Vietnam, as well as in Kwangsi Chuang Autonomous Region, Yunnan, Hunan, Kwangtung and Kweichow Provinces of China. They live by growing a dry, glutinous rice in their mountainous land by the slash-and-burn method. Formerly poppy growers and opium traders, they now produce pigs and peppers for sale, and in lower land soya beans and peanuts as well. Yao who become Christians or Buddhists are strictly speaking no longer Yao – they have 'thrown away the ancestor spirits', and no longer participate in the complex Yao ritual system, though they can still take part in social and economic life. Archaic literary Chinese has been mixed with, and has a central place with, Yao in their ritual. They speak modern Chinese principally only for business reasons.

ZHER-KHIN *Population:* unknown. Language group: unknown. The Zher-khin are a branch of the Na-khi who live on the banks of the Zho-cchu. The word 'zher' means to be afraid, and refers to their being afraid to come from their hot valleys to the snowy upland where the Na-khi live. Zherkin is used as an insulting term for cowardice and stupidity. The Zher-khin use pictographs for their written language. All Zher-khin are expert swimmers, and they transport goods across the Yangtze by using goatskin bags which they tie on their bodies and inflate so that they can float like corks and pull the goods-laden rafts behind them as they swim.

(All population figures are approximate)

ALTERNATIVE NAMES FOR THE PEOPLES OF THE FAR EAST

ALTERNATIVE NAME	NAME	ALTERNATIVE NAME	NAME	ALTERNATIVE NAME	NAME	ALTERNATIVE NAME	NAME
A-nu	Lu-tzu	Jinghpaw	Ching-po	Meo	Miao-tze	P'u	Hsi-fan
Ber Dser	Pai	Jui	Puyi	Miao	Miao-tze	Pu-i	Puyi
Ber Wa Dser	Pai	Kachin	Ching-po	Min-chia	Pai	Pu-yueh	Puyi
Bhutia	Bhote	Kakhieng	Ching-po	Min-chia-tzu	Pai	Rumai	Pulang
B'lai	Li	K'a-la	Wa	Monguor	T'u	Salar	Sa-la
B'li	Li	Kam	Tung	Moso	Nasi	Sho	She
Boa	Hsi-fan	Kamba	Tibetan	Mosu	Lolo	Shui-chia	Shui
Bod	Tibetan	Kao-ch'e	Uighur	Muhso	Lahu	Shui-hu	Puyi
Bodpa	Tibetan	K'a-wa	Wa	Murmi	Tamang	Singhpo	Ching-po
Ch'ao-hsien	Korean	Kei-lao	Ch'i-lao	Musso	Lahu	S'lai	Li
Chingpaw	Ching-po	Kelao	Ch'i-lao	Mussuh	Lahu	Sui	Shui
Ch'ra-me	Hsi-fan	Kha	Chetri	Nachri	Nasi	Ta-hu-erh	Daghor
Chung-chia	Puyi	Kha Lao	Ch'i-lao	Na-hsi	Nasi	Tai Loi	Wa
Dagur	Daghor	Khambu	Kiranti	Na-khi	Nasi	Ta-kuan-erb	Daghor
Dai Dli	Li	Khi Lao	Ch'i-lao	Nashi	Nasi	Ta-kan-erh	Daghor
Daur	Daghor	Khuei	Muslim	Nazo	Nasi	Tangut	Tibetan
Dioi	Puyi, Tai	Kim Mien	Yao	Neisu	Lolo	Thi	Ch'i-lao
Ektharia	Chetri	Kim Mun	Yao	Nesu	Lolo	Thienbaw	Ching-po
Hai	Wa	K'lai	Li	Ngosu	Lolo	Thu	Ch'i-lao
Ha-sa-k'o	Kazakh	K'o-erh-k'o-ssu	Kirghiz	Nin Kam	Tung	T'ou	Lolo
Hei-i	Lolo	Ku-t'ou	Lolo	No	Lolo	Trun	Ch'iu-tzu
Hei Ku	Lolo	La	Wa	Norsu	Lolo	T'u	Chuang
Hiaia	Li	La-bhu	Pai	Nosu	Lolo	Tsang	Tibetan
Hkawa	Wa	La-hu	Lahu	Nu-tzu	Lu-tzu	Tung-chia	Tung
Hkun	Wa	Lai	Li	Nyo	Wa	Tung-jen	Tung
Hmong	Miao-tze	Lai-wa	Wa	O-lo-ssu	Russian	Ughuri	Uighur
Hmu	Miao-tze	Lawa	Wa	Pai-jen	Pai	Uygur	Uighur
Hmung	Miao-tze	Le	Li	Pai-man	Pai	Vu	Wa
Ho	Muslim	Leisu	Lolo	Pain-yu	Pan-yu	Wa Wu	Wa
Houni	Ha-ni	Lingnan	Yao	Palaung	Pulang	Wei-ur	Uighur
Hsi-po	Sibo	Lohei	Laku	Panaka	Tibetan	Wei-wu-erh	Uighur
Hui	Muslim	Loi	Li	Pang-hse	Muslim	Woni	Ha-ni
Hui-hu	Uighur	Loi	Wa	Panthay	Muslim	Wuman	Nasi
Hui-tze	Muslim	Loi-la	Wa	Panthe	Muslim	Wu'tzu-pieh-k'o	Uzbek
Humai	Pulang	Lo-kuei	Lolo	Pei-i	Lolo	Xan Lao	Ch'i-lao
Hwei	Muslim	Luhsi	Nasi	Pen-ti	Puyi	Yao-man	Yao
I	Lolo	Lukhi	Nasi	Per-nu-tuu	Pai	Yi	Lolo
I-chia	Lolo	Man	Manchurian	Per-tsu	Pai	Yoi	Puyi
I-jen	Puyi	Man-chia	Lolo	Pe-tsen	Pai	Yu Mien	Yao
I-lao	Ch'i-lao	Manchu	Manchurian	Pe-tso	Pai		
Iu Mien	Yao	Man-tzu	Lolo	Petsu Shua Ber Ni	Pai		
Jao-chia	Puyi	Meng	Mongols	Piseka	T'uchia		